DOUBLE TAKE
Two sides One story

D0995484

DISCOVERING
DINOSAURS

VALERIE WILDING

For my great friend, Tessa
with love

This story is based, as much as possible, on primary source material - the words and
pictures of the people that witnessed the events described. Whilst it is not possible to
know the exact thoughts, feelings and motives of all the people involved, the book aims
to give an insight into the experience of the events, based on the available evidence.

Scholastic Children's Books
Commonwealth House, 1–19 New Oxford Street,
London, WC1A 1NU, UK
A division of Scholastic Ltd
London ~ New York ~ Toronto ~ Sydney ~ Auckland
Mexico City ~ New Delhi ~ Hong Kong

Published in the UK by Scholastic Ltd, 2003

ISBN 0 439 97333 3

Printed and bound by Nørhaven Paperback, Denmark

Cover image supplied by the Natural History Museum, London

2 4 6 8 10 9 7 5 3 1

The right of Valerie Wilding to be identified as the author of this
work has been asserted by her in accordance with the Copyright,
Designs and Patents Act, 1988.

Contents

Introduction

THIS STORY BEGINS before electricity, before railways, and before anaesthetics, when most people firmly believed that God had created the world in seven days. Before that, there was nothing. God had created Man and every living creature, and people believed that they were the same now as they were when they'd first been created.

Many nineteenth-century churchmen were passionate scientists, eager to investigate God's Earth. Discovering its secrets would, they believed, help them to learn more about God. However, others were forming new theories – that there was some sort of gradual process where life forms did change, or evolve. Charles Darwin, in particular, was developing his own theory – that the fittest creatures survived, and they were the ones who were best adapted for their own particular way of life: the strongest, the fastest, the biggest, and so on.

For centuries, strange bones – huge ones – had occasionally been unearthed. Some ancient people thought they were from dragons, others imagined a race of giants. But new discoveries of monstrous fossils, and the seemingly far-fetched theories of a small group of men, would soon cause people to question their deepest beliefs and understanding.

Some scientists could not accept these findings. One was actually driven mad by his inability to accept the idea that colossal beasts might have roamed the Earth thousands, if not millions, of years before God created Adam and Eve. It shook the very foundations of his religious belief.

Others were convinced the new science would reveal the existence of species long-since extinct, and explain their place in the fascinating story of life on Earth. Two of these men were Gideon Mantell and Richard Owen. Both were equally determined to go down in history for their part in the discovery of dinosaurs...

A Country Doctor
1790–1822

NEARLY A THOUSAND years ago, a noble knight named Mauntell took part in the Norman invasion of England with William the Conqueror. Mauntell's descendants – now known by the name Mantell – thrived and prospered until 1554, when a Walter Mantell made the fatal mistake of getting involved in an uprising against Queen Mary Tudor. He was executed and, as a further punishment, the family lands and fortunes were seized – a hefty fine indeed, since it completely ruined the family.

From then on, the Mantells led a more modest, hard-working existence. None of them was destined to make any particular mark on history. And then, in 1790, a boy named Gideon Algernon Mantell was born in the quiet country town of Lewes, Sussex, in the south of England. His father, Thomas, was a tradesman – a simple shoemaker – but it wasn't long before Mantell heard tales of his more colourful ancestors. As a boy, he used to dream that perhaps he'd grow up to be the one who would restore the family honour.

When he was six, Mantell was sent to a dame school to learn to read and write. Dame schools were small affairs, usually run by an elderly woman, or dame, in her own sitting room. Some women just minded the children and took the money, but it seems Mantell's dame did a good job. She was fond of him, at least, and he soon mastered the basics. More formal education followed a year later, first at a local school called John Button's Academy, and then at his uncle's school in Wiltshire, where he was taught alongside his cousin. He worked hard, by all accounts, was a keen reader, and soon showed a lively interest in natural history.

Once, while barely in his teens, Mantell was walking with a friend along the banks of a stream when he spotted something unusual. He fished it out of the water and ran his hands over it. It had a rough feel to it, yet the shape and markings were too regular for it to be an ordinary lump of rock; it seemed to be coiled in a flattish spiral, like a shell. But the strangest thing was the weight. It was so heavy that it couldn't possibly be an ordinary shell. Curious, his friend came to see and asked if it was a carved stone. Mantell shook his head and said he'd seen something similar in a magazine. *"I think,"* he continued, *"that it is what they call a fossil."* He was right. It was an ammonite – the fossil of an ancient shelled creature. The thrill of his find might well have been the spark that ignited Mantell's passion for geology, and especially for fossils.

At 15, Mantell's schooling was over and he returned home to Lewes. He had to earn a living, so it was time to look to the future. He was apprenticed to a local surgeon called James Moore. His path was set. He would fulfil his apprenticeship and eventually qualify as a surgeon with a diploma from the Royal College of Surgeons. He would become a country doctor, marry, raise a family and live happily ever after. That was the plan.

But Mantell was becoming increasingly enthusiastic for geology. In his spare time, he wandered the local chalk hills of the South Downs looking for fresh fossil specimens until he had a growing collection.

Mantell was only 17 when his father died. This was a dreadful blow for the family but, fortunately, Thomas Mantell had owned valuable property. At least they were provided for. There was even enough to send Mantell to finish his studies in London, where he could get actual experience in the wards of a hospital. So, off he went, a fatherless teenager, to face life in the big city. Naturally, part of his precious collection of fossils accompanied him on the London stagecoach. He was heading for the next step in his career, at St Bartholomew's Hospital – or

Bart's, as it's known – where he attended lectures on anatomy given by the experienced surgeon, Professor John Abernethy.

Mantell worked hard at his medical studies, but geology was fast becoming his first love. He spent his holidays collecting fossils – ammonites, fishes, shells – and continued to read all he could find about the work of the great men of geology, such as William Buckland and James Parkinson, two of the original members of the newly formed Geological Society.

Most people in the early nineteenth century believed the Earth that God had created in seven days was only 6,000 years old. The Reverend Dr William Buckland, eminent geologist and churchman, was no different. The amazing discoveries of a prehistoric world which were to be made over the next 40 years would cause him the greatest grief, as he tried, and failed, to make sense of it all.

James Parkinson, equally well known as a geologist, was also a doctor. Maybe it was this common medical background that gave the young student surgeon Gideon Mantell, now 21, the courage to make an appointment to meet him.

Parkinson welcomed Mantell to his home, and treated him with great courtesy. Mantell was allowed to spend hours poring over Parkinson's own collection, listening intently as the great man talked of how each stratum, or layer, of rock held its own types of fossils, according to age. He continued to give support to Mantell's scientific enquiries for a long while afterwards, too. The kindness and interest shown by this generous man would undoubtedly have spurred Gideon Mantell forward in his quest for knowledge. In fact, he resolved that when he could settle back in Lewes, he would spend all his spare time investigating the *"organic remains of a former world"*.

Little did he realize just what an incredible world he would discover.

In 1811, Gideon Mantell earned his diploma from the Royal College of Surgeons. Shortly afterwards he qualified as a midwife – a term used for both males and females who assisted in childbirth – and was ready to return to Lewes to practise his profession.

James Moore, Mantell's former master, was delighted to invite his ex-apprentice to join his practice, and Mantell soon proved himself an asset. He was hard-working, kind, and an exceptionally gifted midwife who was soon to be delivering two or three hundred babies a year. At that time, childbearing was an event fraught with danger, but Mantell built up an amazing record: it's said that out of over 2,000 mothers he attended, only two died. The practice prospered and it was probably thanks to Mantell's efforts that the profits soon trebled.

Now he was established in a successful practice, and earning a living, Mantell could start thinking about settling down. He was a tall, dark and handsome man, and when he met the equally attractive daughter of one of his patients, love soon blossomed. Mary Ann Woodhouse was a slender brown-haired young woman with large dark eyes. To add to her charms, she showed great interest in fossils, and Mantell became a regular caller at her home, no doubt bringing his latest finds to amaze her.

With this shared interest, the couple were ideally suited and, in May 1816, Mary Ann Woodhouse became Mary Ann Mantell. The young bride – she was only 20 – went to live with her new husband in a rented house in Lewes.

They were a contented pair. Mary Ann would go on fossil-hunting trips with him and, on fine days, accompanied him on many of his visits to patients. While he was inside the house, she liked to wander around outside, keeping her eyes open for anything interesting. It was this habit which would one day produce one of the most celebrated geological finds of the century.

Mantell had already published articles on the geology of the Lewes district, and now he burned to write a book about the geological strata of the South Downs, the ridge of hills stretching across Sussex. The book, Mantell hoped, would make the top men of geology sit up and take notice of him. As a published geological author, he would have earned the right to be treated as a real scientist. Mantell was very aware that, because he hadn't been to university, those scientists who had would consider him a mere amateur. Perhaps, with this book, he would begin to be accepted in the scientific community. He had Mary Ann's total support for the project, and she even offered to try her hand at doing the illustrations.

Mantell must have felt himself very fortunate. His marriage was a true partnership.

Mantell worked hard at his doctor's duties and eventually earned enough to buy the Lewes medical practice from James Moore. He bought a pair of neighbouring houses, which he had joined together into one. The house had a small garden, which nestled into the base of a large mound. On the mound, overlooking the house, stood the keep of Lewes Castle and Mantell gave his new property the grand name of Castle Place. The rectangular columns which adorned the front of the house were each topped by two ammonites as decorations, instead of the usual scrolls. The ammonites weren't put there solely on Mantell's behalf. The builder was called Amon Wilds, and ammonites were a play on his name. Mantell must have felt them most apt, as they seemed to proclaim, "Here lives a geologist!"

So now he was a married man with a thriving practice, and the owner of property. The shoemaker's son was doing well. And more responsibility was to come in 1818 in the shape of Ellen Maria, his first child. She was followed less than two years later by a son, Walter.

The family home was comfortable, and there were servants and assistants to help both Mary Ann and

Mantell. Life was good. Life was full of promise. On his wedding anniversary, he wrote, *"At this moment my domestic happiness is certainly greater than ever."*

In August he noted in his journal that he had visited at least 40 or 50 patients every day for some time: *"yesterday I visited 64 ... our house is like a public office".* Smallpox and typhoid outbreaks were two of the reasons. There were patients to bleed, burns to dress, teeth to pull, even amputations. And at any hour of the day or night, he might be sent for to deliver a baby. He was constantly on call.

How on earth Mantell managed to carry on his profession, build his collection, and do the research and writing for his first book, *Fossils of the South Downs*, is a mystery. It's been said he only had four hours' sleep a night, which isn't difficult to believe. But manage he did. Mantell simply snatched any spare time to go out hunting for more fossils. He'd discovered a quarry in a wooded area known as the Weald, very different from the smooth, rolling South Downs. It was at a place called Whiteman's Green, near Cuckfield in Sussex. Mantell noted the variety of different strata – the layers of rock which had been exposed by quarrying. He also noticed that the fossils in this quarry were different from the ones he'd excavated from the chalk hills around his home. They had been fossils of small sea-creatures, such as starfish, sea-urchins, barnacles and fish. These were bigger.

In fact, many of these fossils were huge. To say

Mantell was intrigued as to what creature they could possibly have come from would be an understatement. So when, in the summer of 1819, he visited a woman in the village of Cuckfield, to examine her late husband's fossil collection, he took the opportunity to go back to the quarry at Whiteman's Green for another look around. He must have been itching to get down and start digging but, just then, a thunderstorm burst overhead and completely ruined the outing. Drenched with rain, Mantell made an arrangement with a quarryman called Leney for interesting fossils to be sent to him at Lewes. That would save him trying to find the time to keep making the long trip to Cuckfield.

This arrangement was to be of the greatest importance to Gideon Mantell, and to the future course of his life. Leney continued to send specimens from Whiteman's Green, and one day, after Mantell had opened the latest batch, he recorded in his journal, *"Received a packet of fossils from Cuckfield; among them was a fine fragment of an enormous bone, several vertebrae and some teeth..."* The fossilized teeth looked rather like those of a crocodile.

Mantell studied the rock layers of Whiteman's Green and gradually came to the conclusion that the strata there were from a lower, older level than the chalk South Downs. Even though they were now at the surface they were, he believed, from the Secondary layers (see diagram on page 16). The fossils coming out of those deeper strata in Whiteman's Green were older than

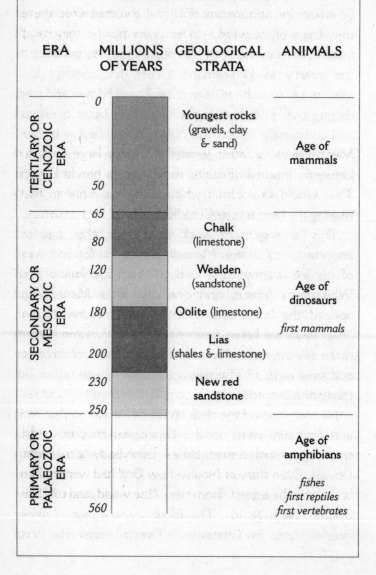

GEOLOGICAL TIMELINE

ERA	MILLIONS OF YEARS	GEOLOGICAL STRATA	ANIMALS
TERTIARY OR CENOZOIC ERA	0 – 50 – 65	Youngest rocks (gravels, clay & sand)	Age of mammals
SECONDARY OR MESOZOIC ERA	65 – 80 – 120 – 180 – 200 – 230 – 250	Chalk (limestone) / Wealden (sandstone) / Oolite (limestone) / Lias (shales & limestone) / New red sandstone	Age of dinosaurs *first mammals*
PRIMARY OR PALAEOZOIC ERA	250 – 560		Age of amphibians *fishes* *first reptiles* *first vertebrates*

anything he'd found before. And, as he'd already discovered, they were bigger, too.

Working on the assumption that the creatures these bones belonged to were in older layers of rock, they must have lived long before the creatures whose fossils he'd discovered around Lewes.

But what were they?

Gideon Mantell's fossils weren't the only large ones to have been found in Britain. A few years previously, in 1812, a Dorset woman named Mary Anning had discovered the fossil skeleton of a huge sea creature, which eventually became known as the ichthyosaur or "fish-lizard". She continued to collect fossils and was visited by great men, such as Dr William Buckland of the Geological Society, intent on pursuing his studies. Many thought the ichthyosaur was more like a crocodile than a fish; it had little baby teeth growing beneath the bigger teeth, which is typical of reptiles. Their teeth are replaced throughout their lives.

So when Mantell found his big fossil bones, he assumed at first that they belonged to an ichthyosaur, and that the land where they were found had once been covered by the sea. It wasn't such a strange idea. Everybody at that time knew the Bible story of Noah – how God had warned him there was to be a great flood over all the world, and told him to build an ark. Noah took his family, and a pair of every living creature, into the ark. While all other life was destroyed, they were saved. As the flood levels went down, Noah was able to release his creatures to start life afresh.

Gideon Mantell knew the Bible well, but he was prepared to look beyond the stories of the Creation and the Flood. He wasn't going to twist and shape the evidence to fit Bible stories, as some scientists did. To him, science – knowledge – was the important thing, not how closely his theories and ideas fitted the Church's thinking. He kept his mind open.

So when, in the same area at Whiteman's Green, Mantell began to find the fossils of plants, and realized he'd stumbled on a bit of a mystery, he put the story of the Flood behind him and investigated further. These ancient plants weren't seaweed. They were land plants. So could his big fossil bones belong to a water-dwelling ichthyosaur? It didn't seem likely now. And then when he discovered a chunk of fossilized tree trunk, over a metre long, in the same place as he was finding bones, the puzzle deepened. He was well and truly stumped. This tree didn't appear to be anything like those which grew around him in the Weald.

Mantell found more and more strange fossilized plants. He couldn't make head nor tail of them, so he decided to go to London and ask an expert. What he found out rather took him aback. The fossils he was finding were of tropical plants. But the south of England certainly didn't have the right kind of climate for those. His chunk of tree, he learned, was from a tree fern, which had a trunk with ferny fronds sprouting from the top – far more likely to be found in tropical lands than growing wild in Britain. What was going on?

He came to the only possible conclusion – that this whole area of southern England had once basked in tropical sunshine. But when? Mantell's finds puzzled him more and more. *"At what period was it ... that turtles and gigantic crocodiles lived in our climate and were shaded by forests of palms...?"* he wondered.

When he eventually saw some scientific illustrations of the ichthyosaur, with detailed descriptions, Mantell realized that the bones he was finding were very different. They were much too thick and heavy for a start. One particular bone which Leney had sent him, for instance, was over 60 centimetres long, and measured 50 centimetres in circumference. And that was only part of the bone. But if it wasn't an ichthyosaur, he wondered, what on earth was it? He hadn't a clue. What he did know was that he was finding more and more gigantic bones and teeth. And they belonged to some completely unknown animal.

Mantell had to find out more. He took a tooth to the Hunterian Museum at the Royal College of Surgeons, where there was a great collection of thousands of anatomical specimens. He asked for the advice of the conservator, or keeper – a man called William Clift. After examination, Clift said he was quite certain the pointed tooth belonged to a reptile, probably a crocodile or a monitor lizard.

Mantell was prepared to accept this. After all, Clift was an expert. But the more he pondered, the more he realized that if it was a monitor lizard or a crocodile, it was a jolly big one – monstrous, in fact. He compared the bigger of his bones with those of an elephant. To his amazement, the so-called lizard would have been as big as the elephant, and would have been more than nine metres long!

A giant fossil reptile ... hardly a normal crocodile! Mantell went home to Sussex with plenty to think about.

One day in 1822, while Mantell was visiting a patient, Mary Ann wandered around outside as usual, keeping her eyes peeled for fossil specimens. This time she came across a heap of broken stone, dumped by road menders. Perhaps she poked among the loose stones with the toe of her boot; it was probably a habit of hers. Maybe the sun glinted on something smooth and shiny. However it happened, she spotted something unusual, picked it up and examined it curiously.

It turned out to be the most exciting find she ever made – although she certainly didn't realize it at the time. For what Mary Ann had picked up was a fragment of tooth, but instead of being long and pointed, like the teeth Leney had sent to Mantell, it was blunt.

Now Mantell had two types of tooth: the sharp, curved ones he'd shown to Clift, and this new, blunt one. A sharp tooth was made for tearing flesh, while this was worn down on one side, which show[e] for chewing. In fact, Mantell wrot[e] *smooth and oblique surface of the crov[n] belonged to an herbivorous animal*". [It may have] been the tooth of a modern hippo or rhino, both of which are plant-eaters, or herbivores. When Mantell discovered that the stones in which it was found had come from the very quarry at Whiteman's Green where his fossil reptile came from, it threw him into confusion. Mammals like the hippo and rhino were frequently found in the more recent Tertiary rock layers above the Secondary strata. If this fossil tooth did indeed belong to a modern mammal, what was it doing in the same ancient layers as the giant, carnivorous, fossil reptile?

No, he reasoned, it could not be from a mammal. Nothing he'd discovered so far seemed to fit. He rejected possibilities one by one and finally arrived at a staggering conclusion. The tooth, he was almost convinced, was from a herbivore. It came from the strata which contained creatures from the age of reptiles – the strata he called the Tilgate Beds, after the local Tilgate Forest. Then it must have come from a gigantic reptile – a gigantic *herbivorous* reptile. But there was no such thing. Was there?

Mantell began to take his ideas a step further when he unexpectedly made the acquaintance of Charles Lyell, a likeable young Scotsman. Lyell was a lawyer by training, but had also studied under William Buckland, who was a professor at Oxford University and Keeper of the Ashmolean Museum. This Scotsman was as crazy about geology as Mantell himself and would, in years to come, give up law completely and devote himself to science. The two men were to become great friends, and Lyell was to have a profound effect on Gideon Mantell's life.

While investigating a quarry earlier that autumn day, Lyell had heard about the local doctor who was also a geologist, and headed over to see if he could take a look at Mantell's fossil collection. He was welcomed with open arms, and the two were, as Mantell wrote to a friend, *"in gossip until morning"*. For a long time, poor Mary Ann Mantell had been putting up with fossils taking over her house, and a more and more preoccupied husband. Now here was a brand new acquaintance keeping him up all night!

It's thought Lyell probably told Mantell that William Buckland, too, had some giant fossil bones, in his care at the Ashmolean Museum. These had been found at a place called Stonesfield, and they were so big that they were known as the Stonesfield Beast. Nobody knew what they really were. An animal? A giant? Visitors to the museum looked at them curiously and went away none the wiser.

What Mantell didn't know was that Buckland was deliberately keeping quiet about the giant bones. The French naturalist Georges Cuvier, famous for his skills in comparative anatomy, had travelled to Oxford from the National Museum of Natural History in Paris. He'd examined the bones, and reckoned the creature they came from was a gigantic, 12-metre-long reptile, previously unknown to man.

Buckland, like all the scientific community, had enormous respect for Cuvier, and he had to consider seriously what the great man said. Cuvier was famed for being able to deduce from the smallest remains exactly what type of creature a particular fossil bone came from. This was because he believed all animal life had characteristics to suit its particular lifestyle. Using his renowned skills, he could build a whole skeleton starting from just a few fossil bones.

But Cuvier's pronouncement profoundly disturbed Buckland. He firmly believed in the Biblical story of creation, and that all life had later been swept away in the Flood. Everything alive today, he reasoned, was a descendant of the life forms on Noah's ark. None of the texts he'd read mentioned any giant reptiles among the passengers. As a scientist and churchman, he desperately wanted to prove that science and the Bible could go hand in hand. He could not accept anything that made it look as if they contradicted each other. Those giant bones weren't helping.

However, Cuvier was keen for Buckland to publish his findings about the Stonesfield Beast, because he wanted to include information about it in his own book. Buckland was going to have to do something very soon. He would have to describe the beast scientifically and name it. If not, someone else might beat him to it.

Once Mantell learned of Cuvier's pronouncement, he could hardly contain himself. Lyell went to the trouble of getting some Stonesfield fossils to send to Mantell, who decided that they were definitely very similar to the ones he'd found at Whiteman's Green. While he was terribly disappointed not to have been the first to discover these huge creatures, at least he was some way towards proving that his belief in ancient gigantic reptiles was not so far off the mark.

There was something that easily compensated for his disappointment. The other tooth, the one his wife had found, belonged to a plant-eating animal. Of that Mantell was sure. It was nothing to do with the Stonesfield Beast, which was clearly a sharp-toothed carnivore. This one was *his* discovery. He, Gideon Mantell the country doctor, would describe the herbivorous reptile for science. By being the first to have his scientific description read before one of the learned societies, and by giving the creature a name, he would become a respected scientist. He would make his own name.

when he was six, he went on to Lancaster Grammar School. His tutors' opinions of him seem to have varied. He got on well with one or two of them, but didn't seem to have impressed another, who called him *"lazy and impudent"*. Though still small and slightly built, Owen was no wimp. He was perfectly happy to get into a fight and, on one occasion, Mrs Owen was extremely put out when another boy, as she complained, *"blacked [her] eldest son's eyes so shockingly"*. Perhaps she wasn't aware that Owen's taunting was the cause of the fight.

Owen must have worked well enough to stick it out at school, because he ended up as one of the first six boys – the top seniors. These were entitled to certain privileges. For instance, there was an ancient custom that whenever a wedding was held in the local church, the first six boys could claim a fee of at least a shilling – a useful sum to a schoolboy – and often more. In the past, they'd had to perform some small part in the ceremony, but nobody bothered with that any more. They got the money just for turning up. One time, though, the bridegroom, a cautious farmer who wanted his money's worth, said he wouldn't pay up until one of the boys would *"gie him a homily"*. Most of the boys would rather forget the money than attempt a sermon, and were all for leaving, but not Richard Owen. He was made of stronger stuff. Taking a step forward, he immediately began to speak to the congregation – in Latin. None of them realized he was simply quoting from his Latin textbook and, as the poor farmer couldn't understand a word, he immediately coughed up the cash. That must have increased Owen's popularity amongst his fellow pupils!

Owen had become a tall, gangly young man, with big dark eyes and a strong chin. At that time, his hobby was heraldry. He found the whole business of coats of arms, and who was entitled to bear them, absolutely fascinating. Owen rather fancied that the next step would be to enter Heralds' College, where he'd already been promised a place by a family friend. Heraldry, he assumed, would eventually become his career. However, the man who'd promised to help him into the college died before Owen could take it up. The place, *"which luckily I did not get,"* he wrote later in life, was no longer open to him.

In 1820, Owen was, like Gideon Mantell, apprenticed to a local surgeon. His master, Leonard Dickson, was surgeon to the county gaol, and it was his job to perform post-mortems on prisoners who had died. Most surgeons didn't have a ready supply of fresh bodies for their apprentices to practise on, so having access to dead prisoners gave great opportunities for students like Owen to get some hands-on experience in practical anatomy.

Owen said he looked forward to his first post-mortem, but *"not without feelings of awe"*. Like many schoolboys of the time, he was steeped in legends of the supernatural. Thoughts of encountering ghosts, or the undead, had been real fears, and now the thought of cutting up a corpse gave him the creeps.

When the big day came, Owen and a senior student were led five storeys up a tall, forbidding tower to the prison hospital and the post-mortem room. A sheet covering the corpse was pulled back. Owen was completely transfixed by the *"pale, cold, collapsed features of the deceased"*. He tried to concentrate on the senior student's explanation of what he was doing, but found himself unable to take his eyes off the *"glassy staring eyeballs"*.

Owen left the gaol that day with *"both appetite and ardour for science somewhat damped"*. He must have seriously questioned whether or not a medical career was right for him.

Then at dusk that evening, with a storm brewing, he was sent back to the gaol to treat a prisoner. As Owen climbed the tower stairs, alone this time, his lantern blew out. Heart pounding, he wanted to fetch another light, but, "No," he said to himself, "they'll think you were afraid to pass the corpse room in the dark." So, terrified, he continued his climb into the blackness.

A sudden gleam of light made him look up. There, clutching the centre pillar of the spiral staircase, was a tall, thin figure. *"My first alarm grew into a creeping and freezing horror,"* Owen said later. He was convinced he could make out the collapsed features and glassy eyeballs of his first corpse. He hurtled back down the stairs, but a second white-clad figure appeared below! In terror he charged past it and, as he did so, felt something move against him. He glanced back, dreading what he would see...

He was dragging a white sheet behind him! His ghosts were nothing more than sheets hung up on the stairway to dry.

As he left, the gaoler eyed him closely and asked what was wrong. Owen simply returned his keys and lantern, looking cool and in control. Inside he was far from cool, but he would never have let the gaoler know that. Did Owen pluck up the courage to go back and treat the prisoner? He never said.

Once outside he swore, all the way home, that never again would he *"desecrate the Christian corpse"*, and that he would leave the medical profession as soon as he could.

It was lucky for science that Richard Owen broke his word.

Within a few months, Owen began to find the work he was doing so absorbing that his interest overcame his squeamishness, and his vow to leave medicine was soon forgotten. His master, Leonard Dickson, noted how skilful and enthusiastic his new pupil had become in so short a time.

Owen took to reading more and more about anatomy, and even began a collection of anatomical specimens of his own, mainly the skulls and skeletons of small animals. He compared one with another, noting differences and similarities between species. It wasn't long before he developed a burning ambition to become a comparative anatomist.

His master, Leonard Dickson, died in 1822, and Owen was transferred to another surgeon by the name of Joseph Seed. When Seed joined the Royal Navy 18 months later, Owen was on the move again, this time to James Harrison, a surgeon and apothecary. In 1824, he was sent to Edinburgh University to continue his anatomical studies.

Professor Monro was Owen's anatomy lecturer. Monro's thinking was hardly up to date, as the notes he used had also been used by his father and grandfather before him. This wasn't good enough for the enquiring mind of Richard Owen so he looked around for someone he could learn more from – someone who had kept bang up to date. He found Dr John Barclay, who held a course on Practical Anatomy, and on Anatomy and Surgery. Owen had to pay extra for this, but his mother, in her frequent letters, was always urging him to let her know when he needed cash. She was proud of her son's progress and was happy to support him through his training, although she worried about him, especially about the fact that his work was a danger to his health. She told him to make a point *"of washing your hands as often as possible in the dissecting room"*. She also prayed he would enjoy *"the regard and approbation of the professors"*.

This he certainly did, for within six months of arriving in Edinburgh John Barclay urged Owen to go to London and study under Professor Abernethy, the top surgeon at St Bartholomew's Hospital.

When Owen left Edinburgh for this next step in his career, he carried with him a letter from Barclay to Professor Abernethy. Owen was heading for the very same hospital and the very same lecture theatre that Gideon Mantell had attended 15 years before. He didn't know what was in the letter he carried, but he was soon to find out just how favourable it was.

Mantell
Strange Teeth
1822–1825

Gideon Mantell's hopes that *Fossils of the South Downs* would propel him to the forefront of science seemed to have a good foundation. Publishing in those days meant getting readers to subscribe – to pay money up front – before the book came out. Mantell was thrilled to have a couple of earls, including the Earl of Egremont from palatial Petworth House in Sussex, on his list. Egremont was known as a patron, or supporter, of learned men and scientists. But the icing on the cake was when Mantell received a letter one May morning, *"announcing that His Majesty had been pleased to command that his name should be placed at the head of my subscription list for four copies"*. George IV was known to be a great supporter of the arts and science, and his patronage would add stature to Mantell's book. When he walked to the office of the *Lewes Journal* to place an ad for it, Mantell's head must have been held high.

Mary Ann, as Mantell's illustrator, had practised her drawing skills for hours on end before she felt she was anywhere good enough to attempt the real thing. It was a massive undertaking for someone so inexperienced, and her husband's almost apologetic words in the book's preface said:

> As the engravings are the first performance of a lady but little skilled in the art, I am most anxious to claim for them every indulgence. I am well aware that the partiality of a husband may render me insensible to their defects.

However, Mary Ann must have been delighted when her illustrations received a favourable mention in a review.

Although he discussed the gigantic fossil reptile bones in the book, Mantell was canny enough not to mention exactly where they were found. But with descriptions of great beasts, and of tropical plant fossils, he managed to give more than a hint of how he was beginning to visualize this prehistoric time. The book received excellent reviews and was swiftly noticed by the scientific community. It didn't make Mantell much money, but he was more than satisfied with its critical acclaim.

Now Mantell turned his attention back to the strange blunt teeth he'd found at Whiteman's Green. In 1822, with a great feeling of anticipation, he took them to a meeting of the Geological Society. Professor Buckland was there, along with William Clift of the Hunterian

Museum. We can only imagine Mantell's excitement as he handed over his precious fossils for them to examine.

That excitement soon turned to dismay when the great men showed little interest, assuring Mantell the teeth might have belonged to a large fish or a mammal. Only one man, Dr Wollaston, supported Mantell's opinion that he had discovered the teeth of an unknown herbivorous reptile, and encouraged him to continue his researches.

Buckland was kind enough to write to Mantell to advise him that the Wealden strata he'd been exploring could not be Secondary ones, but were more recent Tertiary strata, where mammals, like rhinos and hippos, were to be found (see diagram on page 16).

But Mantell was convinced this was wrong. To prove it, he and Lyell explored further afield, and managed to find areas of Secondary strata around Winchelsea and Rye, where the layers of rock were in exactly the same sequence as those of his Tilgate Beds. To their delight, they even found a similar blunt tooth there.

Joyfully, Mantell wrote about it to the Geological Society, but received no reply. Even when Lyell found further proof that the Tilgate Beds were Secondary, by comparison with similar strata on the Isle of Wight, the men at the Geological Society would not accept that the Tilgate Forest area was anything other than Tertiary.

When Mantell learned Charles Lyell was going on a trip to France, he asked him a favour. Mantell had no one else in England to turn to; perhaps the great Georges

Cuvier would look at the strange tooth and bones. Cuvier was the man who'd identified the Stonesfield Beast as a gigantic fossil reptile. Surely he'd be more open-minded than the Geological Society?

Weeks later, Mantell excitedly ripped open the letter containing Cuvier's response. The tooth, the great anatomist declared (having given it little more than a swift glance), was probably from a rhino, and the bones from a hippo's foot.

The news must have absolutely shattered Mantell's dreams. We don't know how he reacted, because pages have been ripped from his journal, and it only resumes on 1 July, 1823, with news of the baptism of his most beloved daughter, Hannah Matilda: *"my sweet child"*.

For years Mantell had been spending all his time on either his medical duties or his fossils and, after the rejection of his herbivorous reptile theory by both the Geological Society and Georges Cuvier, he'd begun to slip into depression. The house was full of fossils, which Mary Ann had been reasonably content to put up with, but now she had a grouchy husband who was becoming quite difficult to live with. The fact of the matter was that the Mantells' marriage was now decidedly rocky.

A slight compensation followed a few months later, when William Buckland showed the bones of his Stonesfield Beast to the Geological Society. Gideon Mantell was in the audience, and with him was his own box of bones which he firmly believed were from the same carnivorous animal. Now they would have a name. He listened eagerly as Buckland announced that, from the size of the thigh bone, Georges Cuvier had pronounced the beast to be 12 metres long.

Mantell did some quick calculations in his head. His fossil thigh bone was twice as big in circumference as Buckland's. It was clearly from a much larger specimen – the beast must be much longer than 12 metres, probably nearer 24 metres! He listened on, hugging this knowledge to himself, and waited for Buckland to name his beast for science.

And then it came. *Megalosaurus!* "Great lizard" – a fitting name for such a giant. During the discussion afterwards, Mantell got to his feet to present his own findings. The listening scientists must have found this information staggering, but perhaps they were also a little cautious in taking the word of a country doctor. Buckland was certainly intrigued enough to visit Mantell at Lewes a few weeks later, to examine the giant thigh bone and vertebrae in peace and quiet. When he finally published the information he'd presented to the Geological Society, Buckland included an acknowledgement to *"the valuable collection of G. Mantell, Esq., of Lewes"*.

Mantell was highly gratified at having his collection admired by such an eminent man, but there wasn't much else that could cheer him just then. In March 1824, on the day he recorded Buckland's visit, he also explained why he hadn't written his journal for months:

> *So unhappily have my days been spent, that I had not*
> *resolution to record mementoes of wretchedness.*

But however low he felt, Mantell wasn't about to give up on his strange blunt fossil teeth. He still believed they belonged to some sort of herbivorous reptile. He wrote a detailed letter to Georges Cuvier, and enclosed several specimens, hoping they wouldn't get just a passing glance this time. He needed more information.

Mantell was rewarded. The package had clearly caught Cuvier's attention, and intrigued him enough to give the teeth a thorough examination. Back came a letter in which Cuvier admitted he was puzzled. Not a carnivore, he was sure, but quite likely a reptile.

> *Have we not here a new animal – an herbivorous*
> *reptile? Some of the great bones that you possess should*
> *belong to this animal which at present is unique of*
> *its kind.*

He went on to advise Mantell to find a jaw with some teeth still attached.

Unique! Mantell must have smiled to himself. He'd been right all along.

Museum Assistant

1825–1830

ALL HIS LIFE, Richard Owen never forgot the *"sense of desolation"* he felt when he arrived in London. He was still only 20, and he didn't know a soul in the city. Crowds of strange faces passed him as he found his way to the famous St Bartholomew's Hospital, armed with nothing but a letter from Dr Barclay.

When Owen entered the lecture hall, he found that Professor Abernethy, distinctly grumpy, had just finished lecturing and was surrounded by students. As soon as he spotted the stranger, the professor demanded, *"And what may you want?"* Owen handed him the letter, but Abernethy barely glanced at it before stuffing it in his pocket. After standing around for a few moments, not knowing quite what to do, Owen eventually gave up and turned to leave. Suddenly he heard his name called and, to his amazement,

Abernethy invited him to breakfast at his home next morning.

Owen was mightily relieved to find the professor somewhat calmer and more pleasant at breakfast. Abernethy had also had a chance to digest the contents of Barclay's letter and now had the opportunity to take a good look at the young man before him.

To Owen's complete astonishment, he walked out of the house with a job! He was to be prosector for Professor Abernethy's lectures. This meant he was the assistant responsible for dissection and preparation of the human or animal remains, ready for lectures. Now Owen could take advantage of the best teaching in London, and he had access to plenty of bodies for dissection. What's more, they wouldn't cost him a penny.

Professor and assistant got on well, as long as Owen did the job properly. Abernethy had a short fuse. Once, while Owen was preparing a human kidney, he lopped a bit off by accident. No problem, he thought. He stuck it back on and relaxed as Abernethy launched into his lecture. Suddenly the professor stopped and turned to glare at his assistant. Owen must have known instantly that something was amiss. It certainly was – he'd carefully fixed the broken-off bit to the wrong end of the kidney. Owen's grandson later recalled his grandfather telling him that when Abernethy discovered the mistake, *"he did not let the occasion pass without bestowing a few flowers of speech upon his young friend"*.

The quality of Owen's work, however, outweighed any shortcomings, and Professor Abernethy was one of those who supported his membership of the Royal College of Surgeons in 1826. Richard Owen was now a qualified surgeon.

A medical practice of his own was the next step, and Owen soon set up in Cook's Court, Lincoln's Inn Fields, in the heart of London's law district and close to the college.

The Hunterian Museum at the Royal College of Surgeons, where Mantell had asked William Clift to help identify his fossil tooth, was in quite a state. It had originally been the collection of a man named John Hunter, and the specimens were supposed to be exhibited to the public. However, many of Hunter's papers had gone missing, so before anyone could be let in to see the collection, every single item had to be carefully identified and catalogued. William Clift, the conservator, was finding the job an uphill task, and he was making terribly slow progress with the cataloguing. He needed an assistant to concentrate on the work, everyone agreed, but who was up to the job?

Professor Abernethy reckoned he'd found the answer. His ex-assistant, Richard Owen, the passionate anatomist and skilled dissector, was just the chap. He lived nearby, and it would have been very clear to him that time spent on this undertaking would be time well spent. It meant more money for a start but, equally important, Owen would now be right in the centre of the London medical community.

There was someone else working at the Hunterian Museum, too. William Clift's son, William Home Clift, was his chief assistant, and it was understood that when Clift died, William Jr would become conservator. So it was with little expectation of advancement that Owen began his mammoth task of cataloguing the Hunterian collection.

However, Clift also had a daughter, Caroline. She and Owen met in odd circumstances. Caroline had made a pair of decorative bell-pulls, which had to be attached to a wire so they could be pulled to summon a servant. She was on a step-ladder, hanging them, when she slipped and fell badly, almost knocking herself senseless. William Jr yelled for Owen, who came running. His bedside manner must have captivated her, because it wasn't long before they were seeing each other regularly.

A courtship in 1827 had to be conducted in the proper manner, and Owen was up against it from the start, because Caroline's mother wasn't too sure about him. Mrs Clift was determined her daughter's future husband should have a good income and excellent career prospects before wedding bells were allowed to ring.

By the end of the year, Richard Owen and Caroline were engaged, but he couldn't even think of marriage until he'd improved his lot. He became a lecturer on comparative anatomy at Bart's but that didn't bring in much money and he could hardly make much progress at the Hunterian Museum, because of Clift's son. Owen decided the only thing to do was to take a job somewhere else, where he might be able to make a few

41

good career moves. He settled on a position as house surgeon at a hospital in Birmingham.

Things didn't work out for Owen, and he soon wrote to Caroline admitting it. Knowing this wasn't going to make him shine in Mrs Clift's eyes, he craftily ended his letter, *"God bless you, my love, and kiss your mother for me."*

Owen then had to write to William Clift, hoping to smooth his path back to the Hunterian Museum. He clearly thought it best to come clean, so admitted his mistake, and said he was ashamed of his *"stupid self, who ought to have staid at home and minded my bottles"*.

In January 1830, he returned to resume work on the Hunterian collection, and to build up his own medical practice. He also worked at dissecting some of the animals that died at London Zoo. For a comparative anatomist, this was a rich source of knowledge to be tapped, and he took full advantage of any opportunity that came his way.

Owen plodded on, and by 1830 he was publishing the first parts of the Hunterian catalogue. Proudly, he sent a copy to his old master, the surgeon, Joseph Seed, who sent back a prophetic reply, telling Owen, *"You have estimable merit and must shine in the profession, provided your good sense keep it, under all circumstances of fortune, under proper government."*

Richard Owen was indeed to shine, and the next step in his climb to fame was a visit to England by the renowned French naturalist Georges Cuvier – the man who had given Gideon Mantell such longed-for hope.

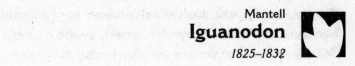

Mantell
Iguanodon
1825–1832

GIDEON MANTELL NOW wanted to compare the teeth
and bones of his herbivorous giant with those of modern
reptiles, to see if he could get any more clues as to what
it might have looked like. He headed for where he knew
there were thousands of anatomical specimens from all
over the world – the Hunterian Museum. William Clift
and he searched for hours through all the drawers of
reptile jaws and teeth, but without success. Then a man
who'd been helping them suggested he show Mantell the
skeleton of an iguana he'd been preparing.

This was what Mantell had been looking for. The iguana
was the closest thing he'd seen to his own fossils. On
comparing the size of the teeth, he worked out that his
prehistoric animal must have been easily 21 metres long.
And since the fossil teeth were so like those of the iguana,
Mantell called his creature *Iguanodon* – "iguana tooth".

In his spare time over the next three or four months, Mantell completed a scientific paper with all the details of his discovery. He decided to bypass the Geological Society and instead present his findings to the Royal Society – the oldest scientific society in the country. Perhaps he felt the Geological Society had discouraged him far too much. So, in February 1825, Mantell's paper was read before the members of the Royal Society by the vice-president. It was called "Notice on the *Iguanodon*, a newly discovered fossil reptile, from the sandstone of Tilgate Forest". It was the first published description of the *Iguanodon* and in it he described how he'd come to the conclusion that what he'd found was an ancient herbivorous reptile.

The paper was very well received and in no time at all Mantell was elected a member of the Geological Society council. Before the year was out, Cuvier himself commented in print on the discovery of the herbivorous reptile, and Mantell was elected an honorary member of the Institute of Paris and a Fellow of the Royal Society. His nomination for election to the Royal Society was signed by, among others, Professor Abernethy, who had taught both Mantell and Richard Owen, and by William Clift, Owen's employer. Things were going well for Mantell but, by the end of the year, he commented that although he had these honours, and he'd even increased his medical practice, *"my strength and health have more than decreased in proportion"*. His heavy workload and overwhelming involvement in geology meant he spent little time with his family, and this was putting a heavy strain on the marriage. Mantell was tired and unhappy. He lists one ailment after another in his journal: a hernia caused by his horse suddenly starting, rheumatism, lumbago, bladder problems ... it went on and on, and he was still only in his mid-thirties.

Over the next couple of years, Gideon Mantell continued writing books about the geology of his native county. He had a fourth child, Reginald, and became so busy, professionally, that he had to take on a partner for the medical practice. With more time to spare for his family and his fossils, the collection grew, too. There were exciting finds, like the femur, tibia and fibula [leg bones] of an *Iguanodon*. But there were frustrations, too, like a massive whale bone, nearly three metres long and about 75 centimetres in circumference...

In attempting to remove it it fell into a hundred pieces! A few fragments were the only relics I could bring away of this, the most magnificent fossil I ever discovered.

Mantell's collection grew as he gathered fossils and casts of fossils from places other than Sussex. Soon, there was so much that he was forced to build a new room on top of his house, with a window overlooking Lewes Castle at the rear. This was to be his geological museum. By the summer of 1829, Mantell was busy moving the collection in, and in September there was an official opening with a grand tea, dancing and then supper.

He was now accepted by the top people in science. William Buckland read a paper to the Geological Society about the *Iguanodon* discoveries, acknowledging the fact that they owed all they knew about the giant herbivorous reptile to Mantell. This must have given Mantell considerable satisfaction, after having had his ideas snubbed by that very society. Another geologist, called Bakewell, visited him at home, and Mantell later recorded in his journal, *"He says I shall ride on the back of my Iguanodon into the temple of Immortality!"*

Mantell was now a Fellow of the Royal Society, a loved and respected doctor and family man – he should have felt on top of the world. Strangely, he felt dissatisfied with his own worth. On his fortieth birthday, in 1830, he wrote,

How very little I have done, and how trifling my scientific acquirements to what I had hoped to have attained long ere I reached this period of existence.

He must have been frustrated that his work as a doctor took up such a great slice of his life. If only he had more time, if only his health didn't keep letting him down and if only things were more settled at home, there was so much he could still achieve. Mary Ann was getting more and more fed up. There were fossils everywhere, there was a constant stream of museum visitors tramping through the house and climbing the narrow staircase leading up to the museum. To cap it all, her husband wasn't showing much attention to her or the children.

But Mantell still pressed on. He knew now that there had been a time when the Earth was populated by unimaginably huge beasts, and that this reptilian age had been long before the age of mammals – and of mankind. He had an idea of the *order* of things from where the fossils were being found – the mammals in strata above the reptiles, for instance – but he still had no idea of just how long ago it all was.

In August 1830 Georges Cuvier visited London. Mantell was feeling highly honoured and very excited because the great anatomist had promised to visit him at Lewes. It's easy to imagine the dreadful disappointment when Mantell opened a letter, one Sunday morning, saying that Cuvier had to leave for Paris shortly and couldn't make it to Sussex.

Well, this opportunity was not going to pass by if Gideon Mantell had anything to do with it. *"I immediately determined to go and see him,"* he wrote, *"and having hastily packed up a box full of fossils ... took my place in the coach to London."* He met his son, Walter, who was in London visiting his grandmother, then stopped overnight at his in-laws' home, and was up at seven the next morning ready to call on Cuvier. At nine, he was shaking hands with his hero – *"the idol of my* scientific idolatry" – and they were soon deep in fossil talk. Mantell left with a promise that Cuvier would come to Lewes in the spring.

Mantell's hopes were built up again in October 1830. George IV had died, and his brother William was now king. He and the Queen were to pay a visit to Lewes. Mantell immediately had some of his books beautifully bound and sent them to the palace. To his joy, he was told the royal couple wished to visit his museum. He, his assistant, Mary Ann and their servants made sure everything was perfect for the royal visitors. Mantell knew that not only would this raise his own profile – it was bound to be in the newspapers – but it would also raise the profile of the science of geology.

But nobody came. Royal walkabouts weren't as finely organized then as they are now, and the King and Queen got a bit behind. A message was sent to the museum saying they'd like to come another time.

Bitterly disappointed, Mantell grabbed a copy of his friend Horsfield's *History of Lewes*, to which he had contributed, and went to find the VIPs. A friend managed to get him presented to the King. Mantell went down on one knee and offered the book with a short speech. *"His Majesty almost interrupted me,"* Mantell wrote that evening, *"with 'Certainly, certainly, much obliged, much obliged', and turning to the Lord in waiting said in his usual hasty manner 'take them, take them'."*

On this occasion there was only a vague suggestion that the Mantells would be honoured by a future visit.

Owen
The Pearly Nautilus
1830–1832

CUVIER'S VISIT TO LONDON was an exciting time for Richard Owen, too. He'd worked hard at cataloguing the Hunterian collection, and had proved himself to be highly skilful and efficient in William Clift's eyes. He was gaining tremendous experience and was engaged to his boss's daughter. And he was in the thick of the scientific community, seeing all, hearing all.

In normal circumstances, Cuvier might not have taken notice of a lowly assistant, might not even have been introduced to him, but Owen had two skills which were to prove invaluable during the visit. Cuvier barely understood a word of English, which made it extremely difficult for him to discuss specimens or current developments with other scientists. However, Owen, whose mother was part-French, had learned the language well, and spoke it almost fluently. On top of that, he'd been gaining a good all-round knowledge of the exhibits in the museum, and was able to interpret freely for Cuvier. *"I made Cuvier's personal acquaintance ... and was specially deputed to show and explain to him such specimens as he wished to examine,"* he wrote.

Although Owen did add modestly that *"there was no special merit in my being thus deputed, the fact being that I was the only person available who could speak French,"* his chest must have swelled with pride at being seen by distinguished scientists chatting with the internationally famous Georges Cuvier.

While Mantell had to be content with the promise of a future visit from Cuvier, Owen was invited to visit the great man himself, in Paris. So, in July the next year, he took advantage of the opportunity and sailed on a steamer to France for a stay of over a month.

Owen had a wonderful time seeing the sights and attending Cuvier's Saturday evening gatherings, known as soirées. He saw King Louis-Philippe, visited the theatre and even took cello lessons. Most of his mornings, though, were spent in the National Museum of Natural History. He had huge admiration for this wonderful institution, devoted to nothing but natural history. What might he achieve, he must have wondered, with a huge and extensive collection like that behind him? Cuvier had every resource available to him. No wonder he had such vast experience, such a wealth of knowledge. No wonder he was such a famous anatomist.

Back in London, Richard Owen moved his medical practice to nearby Symond's Inn and began work on a paper that was to bring him great acclaim: "Memoir on the Pearly Nautilus", finished in 1832. It was translated into French but, sadly, Georges Cuvier would never read it. He died suddenly in May of the same year.

Owen's anatomical investigation of this shelled creature, the pearly nautilus, was described as *"one of the most interesting additions to natural science that has been made for some time"*. Buckland himself described his method of investigation as being *"most able and masterly"*. Praise indeed for a humble museum assistant.

But no one can live on praise alone, and Owen still found Caroline's mother to be an awkward obstacle to his wedding plans. He was desperate to marry, and he searched around for ways to increase his income and prospects. However, events overtook him when a sudden tragedy seemed to solve his problems at a stroke.

In September 1832, William Clift had a few weeks away from his work at the Hunterian Museum. He was travelling from place to place, no doubt visiting friends and private collections. While in Sussex, he spent some time with Gideon Mantell before moving to his next stop on the Isle of Wight. It gave him a chance to catch up on the latest additions to the little museum in Lewes and to discuss the latest discoveries with Mantell.

Little did Clift realize he would soon be called back to London. His son, William Home Clift, had hired a hansom cab – a two-wheeled carriage – to take him home after an evening out. Turning out of Fleet Street, the driver took a corner too sharply. The cab overturned, throwing William out. He landed on his head, and was rushed to St Bartholomew's Hospital where who should be called to attend him but his colleague, Richard Owen.

William's skull was fractured, and Owen could do nothing to save him. His father was tracked down on the Isle of Wight, but it took a while to get word to him. He was only able to make it back in time to be with his son as he died.

The Clifts were grief-stricken, and Owen, who'd been involved with the family for over five years, must have shared their misery. Owen worked harder than ever now and, within a short while, received a 50 per cent salary increase. His prospects had suddenly brightened. Now that William, who was to have stepped into his father's shoes as conservator, had died, Owen was Clift's most likely successor. Surely Mrs Clift could have no objection to her daughter marrying a man who would, in all probability, end up in the same position as her own husband ... one day.

Owen felt that with Cuvier dead, with his increased security at the Hunterian Museum of the Royal College of Surgeons, with highly respected published work to his credit, his path was clear. He was going up. Richard Owen intended to become the British Cuvier.

The "Mantell-piece"
1832–1834

MEANWHILE, GIDEON MANTELL was totally occupied investigating yet another interesting find. Quarry workers in the Tilgate Forest had been blasting away at a large block of extremely hard stone when they spotted fragments of fossilized bone in some of the smaller, broken-off chunks. Knowing from experience that they were in for a nice reward, they put the rocks aside and sent a message to Lewes. As soon as Mantell heard the news, he hurried to the quarry. He examined the rocks and, with mounting excitement, made arrangements for delivery to his home of all the huge lumps of rock that looked as if they might contain fossils.

There were now regular deliveries of fresh rocks, and Mantell would immediately grab his hammer and chisel and start chipping away at them, often till after midnight. Every new fossil that was painstakingly extracted from the rock was put on show for the ever-increasing stream of visitors. Mary Ann must often have felt she wasn't being considered at all, and that Mantell was neglecting her and their children.

But her husband was blind to domestic problems and difficulties. Once he had exposed parts of the animal, Mantell realized he'd been wrong in assuming that this was another *Iguanodon*, or a *Megalosaurus*. He had something new on his hands. Another fossil reptile, unknown to man. He became utterly absorbed in exposing it from the rock.

Gideon Mantell was going to be the one to describe and name this creature. He determined to do so as quickly as possible, and worked day and night with hammer and chisel, chipping away at the rock in which it was entombed. William Clift visited him during this period, on his way to the Isle of Wight, just before the death of his son. Perhaps he was privileged to see parts of the new discovery before any of the geologists.

Mantell uncovered 15 vertebrae, some ribs and about ten strange bony shapes – some over 40 centimetres long, and up to 18 centimetres wide at the base. Could they be some form of armour, he wondered?

Towards the end of the year, the new fossils were ready for display, his paper was written, and Mantell was ready to present his giant fossil reptile to the world. On the last day of November, he sent the fossils to London, and on

5 December 1832, he read his paper to a full house at the Geological Society.

Two things marred the occasion. The first was being told to cut the paper by about a third, *"which was a very great annoyance, at so short a notice"*, because it was going to go on too long. Nevertheless, it was with great pride and satisfaction that he announced to the world the *Hylaeosaurus*, or "forest lizard". *Hylaeosaurus* eventually became known as the first of the armoured dinosaurs, or ankylosaurs, to be discovered.

The second annoyance was the strange reaction of Professor Buckland. Mantell was dismayed when, at the end of his reading, Buckland stood up and picked holes in his paper. He insisted, and wouldn't have it that there was any doubt in the matter, that the strange bony shapes were part of the *Hylaeosaurus*'s back, and not armour at all. He would not budge on this, even though other anatomists present didn't agree with him. Mantell was *"hurt beyond measure"* at the way Buckland reacted, especially as Mantell *"had that very morning sat up till past three to assist him!"*

Buckland had been working on two of the twelve volumes of the *Bridgewater Treatises*. These books, commissioned by the Earl of Bridgewater, were intended to illustrate *"the power, wisdom, and goodness of God as manifested in the Creation"*. Buckland's sections were on geology and mineralogy. He'd finally had to accept that the evidence proved there actually was life before mankind. Now he was having great difficulty in explaining why God had created these hideous carnivorous giants, and his conclusion was that they'd been put on Earth to make sure other creatures had an easy death. He reckoned that when a great beast suddenly pounced on a sick, weak or injured creature and savaged it to death, it was really doing the poor thing a kindness and helping it to heaven. A quick death with just a moment's agony, he reasoned, was much better than suffering and dying slowly, and it made sure the world was full of happy, healthy animals. In this way, Professor Buckland felt that science was in accord with God's great plan.

The night before his lecture Mantell had visited Buckland and had been helping him revise parts of his latest book. He would almost certainly have discussed his new *Hylaeosaurus* with his friend. Maybe the image of a huge armoured beast, suggesting something other than a merciful killer, had been too much for Buckland to accept.

Fortunately, Mantell's opinions were well supported by all the comparative anatomists at the meeting, including William Clift and Richard Owen. Buckland apart, the evening was a triumph for Mantell, and there was much talk about him and his impressive work. He was exceptional, they thought; a *"prodigy"*.

Over the next weeks, Mantell went on to complete a 400-page book called *The Geology of the South-East of England*, describing his recent discovery of the *Hylaeosaurus* and explaining more about the geology of Sussex. But after all that hard work, Mantell was absolutely livid when his usual publisher decided not to print this book. *"After keeping it three weeks!"* he fumed. *"So much for the delights of authorship!"* It infuriated him that so much time had been wasted while the book languished on the publisher's desk. Fortunately, Bakewell, the good friend who had prophesied that *Iguanodon* would make him immortal, sent it to another publisher, with the encouraging comment that Gideon Mantell was *"the British Cuvier"*.

Bakewell's intervention did the trick. Before the book was printed, however, Mantell received a letter which, while putting him into a fever of excitement, also put him in a very embarrassing situation. The writer announced that the King wished Gideon Mantell's new book to be dedicated to His Majesty. What a glorious honour for the son of a shoemaker!

But the trouble was that Mantell had already agreed to dedicate the book to Sir Henry Halford! *"What a hobble..."* was how he described this awkward situation in his journal. Sir Henry was an important man, being President of the College of Physicians. Fortunately, he was also the King's own physician and was probably as aware as anyone that if the King asked, the King received. And so the book bore a dedication to *"His Most Excellent Majesty William the Fourth ... by His Majesty's faithful and devoted Subject and Servant the Author"*.

Mantell was now mixing with high society. He attended grand meetings and functions, such as a conversazione (a social gathering where science, art, literature and so on were discussed) at Kensington Palace, where more than 400 men – *"the most distinguished in science, literature and rank"* – were present. Mantell must have now considered that he was, at last, one of them. He was way in front of all others in knowledge and experience of the newly discovered fossil reptiles.

But there was one thing which Mantell needed above all else: time. How could he make further scientific progress when so many hours in the day were taken up by his practice? *"I sleep but little and wear my eyes dim,"* he wrote, *"yet I can scarcely ever devote an hour to my favourite pursuit."*

The answer, Mantell thought, lay in the seaside resort of Brighton on the south coast. Royalty were frequent visitors there, and wherever royalty went, the wealthy members of society followed. Brighton was the place to be. If Mantell could start a practice there, he could charge much higher fees and could therefore manage with fewer patients. Fewer patients would mean more time for his fossil reptiles.

Although it seemed a great idea, he still dithered. He was now in his forties, with four children to support. Making a drastic move like this, leaving his currently flourishing medical practice, could be disastrous.

Then everything changed. One bright autumn morning Mantell called on the 82-year-old Earl of Egremont, who had been so supportive of him in the past. They chatted for a bit, and he told Egremont what he was thinking of doing. The Earl clearly agreed it was a good idea, because he encouraged him to move and, as Mantell wrote in delight, *"offered me a thousand pounds to assist me in the removal"*.

With that hugely generous gesture, Mantell's mind was made up. Just before Christmas 1833, the Mantells moved into 20, The Steyne. This was a tall, narrow six-storey house right in the thick of fashionable Brighton. The house was expensive, but Mantell had a plan. He established his museum on the drawing-room floor, which can't have pleased Mary Ann. The drawing room itself was light and airy, with tall bay windows and a narrow balcony overlooking the Royal Pavilion to the right and the open sea to the left. Mantell intended to charge visitors to come and see his museum. That would provide a steady trickle of income, which would definitely help offset some of the cost of the grand new house.

However, his friends insisted that charging for entry would be a bad move. It was unprofessional, they said. Science for science's sake, they reckoned, not for money. Regretfully, he decided they were right, and opened the museum, free of charge, on Tuesdays.

The new venture was a terrific success. Visitors flocked to see Gideon Mantell's strange exhibits. There was a constant stream of titled people, important people, scientists – by the beginning of May, he recorded that almost a thousand had passed through the door. And, which must have irritated Mary Ann even more, not always on Tuesdays. After all, Mantell's museum was unique, and nobody wanted to miss it, especially if they were just passing through Brighton. Where else in the whole world could you see fossils of a *Megalosaurus*, an *Iguanodon*, and the newly discovered *Hylaeosaurus*?

Mantell was in demand for lectures; he'd been busy publishing a catalogue describing his exhibits; everything was wonderful. Yet something had to suffer. *"I have scarcely had breathing time, and not one moment of quiet that I could devote to the solitude of my thoughts,"* Mantell confided to his journal. When he did get time to think, the most pressing worry on his mind was his medical practice. Frighteningly, it was almost non-existent.

At the beginning, he wasn't too bothered. *"I have no right to complain at present, time and exertion will yet do much for me,"* he wrote. And there was always the remainder of Egremont's money to keep them going until patients started to turn up.

But they didn't turn up. *"As usual ... hosts of visitors but no patients!"* This was bad news. Without an income from his medical practice, how long could he continue to run the house, the museum – and support his family? Mantell was literally worried sick. He frequently recorded different illnesses in his journal including a stomach infection and excruciating neuralgia [severe nerve pain].

Then in May 1834 there was a new excitement, which must have bucked his spirits up tremendously. A man called William Harding Bensted had unearthed a slab of rock in a quarry near Maidstone. The slab contained some strange brown fragments. Bensted realized they were bits of bone from a huge creature, and had his men search around and collect up all they could find. Being a bit of a fossil-collector himself, Bensted had heard of Mantell, and he wrote to tell him about it.

Mantell, with a friend called William Saull, went to see the slab. He soon identified the bones as being from an *Iguanodon* and, after some friends in Brighton had clubbed together and bought it for him, took it home and began work on it. *"I am chiselling all night,"* he wrote. Now he was beginning to get an idea of what the *Iguanodon* actually might have looked like. The hind feet, for instance, he could tell were *"very large, flat and enormously strong"*. There were teeth buried in the rock, too. Sadly, there was still no jaw, but this was nevertheless a very important find indeed. It was the first time *Iguanodon* bones and teeth had ever been found together.

By September, Mantell had finished chiselling it out and had put it in the museum. It was spectacular, and soon became known as the "Mantell-piece". With a new attraction, visitors positively swarmed to the house, which can't have pleased the long-suffering Mary Ann. Her husband's star was rising, and respect for the brilliant young country doctor grew steadily. But all was not well at home.

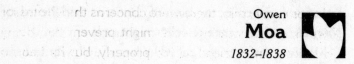

RICHARD OWEN'S STAR was rising, too. Because of his position at the Royal College of Surgeons, he was at the cutting edge of scientific discoveries. He attended meetings of the learned societies and absorbed all the details of other men's amazing investigations and achievements. At the Geological Society, for instance, he heard Gideon Mantell talk about his recent find, the *Hylaeosaurus*. Owen would have noticed how, with each fresh breakthrough, Mantell's reputation and standing grew. The whole business of these fossil reptiles seemed to be a big new area of discovery. It interested him very much indeed.

Owen was still the assistant conservator at the Hunterian Museum, and was now appointed Professor of Comparative Anatomy at Bart's Hospital. Early the next year he was elected a Fellow of the Royal Society.

The certificate described him as *"a gentleman intimately acquainted with Physiology, Comparative Anatomy and the various branches of Natural History"*.

In some quarters, there were concerns that Professor Owen's extra lecturing work might prevent him doing his Hunterian cataloguing job properly, but he had no such fears. He was a hard worker, highly intelligent, and he knew his own capabilities. As if to prove he was more than equal to the task, Owen promptly published further parts of the Hunterian catalogue.

All this recognition went a long way towards proving to Mrs Clift that her daughter's fiancé had a blossoming career. She could hardly deny now that he would be a worthy husband. To the joy of Owen and Caroline, Mrs Clift finally gave the marriage her blessing, and the date was set. The wedding was to take place on 20 July 1835 – Owen's birthday.

Meanwhile, Owen was given an apartment at the Royal College of Surgeons. Once he was installed there, he invited the Clift family to tea. Caroline liked the building, which she knew well. As for the apartment, she thought the downstairs rooms and the kitchen would suit her fine. But, she wrote, *"the upstairs is most inconvenient"*. However, from a financial point of view, the apartment was very convenient indeed, as it meant they could live quite cheaply. It also meant the newlyweds would have a large enough home, in a building impressive enough even for Mrs Clift.

The wedding was small and quiet. Caroline wrote in her diary that after they left the church, *"Caroline Clift having been lost on the road, Mrs Richard Owen returned to breakfast at No. 1 Euston Grove"*, her parents' home.

Richard Owen was now son-in-law and chief assistant to the conservator of the Hunterian Museum, and it wasn't long before he was heir to the post.

Living in part of the building where Owen worked had the same drawback for Caroline as for Mary Ann Mantell: her ambitious husband was happy to work into the small hours. She described one night when *"Richard spent the evening in examining some of the minute worms found in the muscles of a man"*. Fortunately, he did this after dinner.

Although there was plenty going on in Brighton, Mary Ann had the responsibility of a family and little money to spend on fine clothes. Caroline, however, was better off financially and had the benefit of living in London. The Owens had all the entertainments and amusements they could wish for practically on their doorstep. They would frequently spend evenings at concerts or the theatre, and there were daytime outings together, too, very often to the zoo. Owen liked to be seen about town.

Caroline, like Mary Ann, would sometimes do drawings for her husband. She had to put up with his kindly criticism, and once wrote about spending the whole day drawing a wombat's brain for Owen. When he came in, *"he said it was all wrong, so I must do it over again"*.

In April 1836, Owen's career took another step forward, when he was appointed Hunterian Professor at the Royal College of Surgeons. This required him to give a series of lectures, which were named after John Hunter himself. He was forever grateful for this opportunity, because it gave his career such a boost. Professor Owen was suddenly high-profile, and his standing in the scientific world immediately shot up. When he wrote to accept the post, he acknowledged that having access to the Hunterian collection itself had enormously increased his experience of comparative anatomy.

Delivering the lectures was rather nerve-racking, though. Owen once wrote to tell his mother about the formality of the *"somewhat awful affair"* when, after members and students were seated, the clock would strike four and the council and honoured guests would process in, with a mace being carried before them. Finally he, the learned Hunterian Professor would walk in. An hour later, he told her, *"your obedient and affectionate son makes his bow and exit, with a much lighter heart than when he entered"*.

Owen's luck continued when it was agreed the Hunterian Professor should be the one to have access to *all* the animals that died at London Zoo. This was an opportunity for discovery that he simply couldn't get anywhere else – the chance to dissect and examine a steady supply of all sorts of freshly dead creatures. It would cost anyone else an absolute fortune, even if they were able to lay their hands on such a source of knowledge.

To cap it all, Charles Lyell wrote to invite Owen to a party, where he would meet Charles Darwin, just back from a long voyage on the *Beagle*. Darwin had been to South America, Lyell said, *"where he has laboured for zoologists as well as for hammer-bearers"*, meaning fossil-hunters, and was making large donations of animals to the Zoological Society. It was like handing them to Richard Owen on a plate. But although Owen was to work on the fossil animals in co-operation with Charles Darwin, the two men were destined never quite to see eye to eye. At this time, Owen still sided with those, like Buckland, who believed that as each species had been created by God, so it stayed, in that same form. He did not accept the evolutionists' ideas, that life forms changed and developed over millions of years.

In spite of all his extra responsibilities, Richard Owen had made superb progress in cataloguing the Hunterian collection. Everything was now ready to be exhibited. Owen would almost certainly have thought back to his visits to Cuvier's national museum. England still had nothing to match that, but he intended that the Hunterian should be something to be proud of.

Richard Owen was riding high. He was well known, well respected and, with the vast experience he was gaining from working on Darwin's fossil mammals, he was considered a leader in the field of comparative anatomy. He had made a happy marriage, which was also helping to further his career. William Clift would not only hand on his position to his son-in-law when he died, he would also prove influential on his behalf very soon.

On 6 October 1837, Owen's family increased. He made an entry of his own in his wife's diary: *"At a quarter past nine William Owen was born."* Although both Caroline and the baby – to be known as Willie – were well, the poor father was suffering from agonizing toothache, which rather spoiled his excitement.

Owen often managed to find time to spend with young Willie, once recording how two titled gentlemen turned up one day and, to their great amusement, found him attempting to feed the baby.

Everything was going well. Owen had a warm family around him, and honours still continued to turn up. The following February, the Geological Society gave him the Wollaston Gold Medal for his work on Charles Darwin's fossils, and for his geological work generally. The only cloud was his mother's poor health. She wrote rarely now and, although he visited her as often as he was able, he must have missed her letters, which were always full of love, concern and deep admiration. In November 1838, just a few weeks after Owen's return from a long trip to Germany, his sisters wrote to warn him his mother was fading. He immediately hurried to Lancaster, and was relieved and glad to find she was still conscious when he arrived. It wasn't long, though, before she slipped into a final sleep and died. The funeral was a sad affair. Mrs Owen had outlived her friends, and there were only a few members of her family to mourn her.

The sun soon shone again on Richard Owen, who was now spoken of in some quarters as *"the first anatomist of the age"*. There was another project on the horizon which was to bring him more fame than even he imagined. At about this time, the fairly new British Association for the Advancement of Science (BAAS) was growing fast, and committee members wanted to raise the association's profile. What better subject to bring it to the world's attention than the amazing new British discoveries – the giant fossil reptiles?

After lots of discussion, the committee decided to commission someone to write a ground-breaking paper to present to their members, and then to publish. It would be called "Report on the Fossil Reptiles of Great Britain".

But who would they choose to prepare the report? Gideon Mantell? He'd been the one to discover two out of three of the known giant fossil reptiles: *Iguanodon* and *Hylaeosaurus*. But he was a busy country doctor, not often in London. He certainly wasn't a regular at the association's own meetings. In fact, he wasn't seen that often at any of the other learned societies' meetings. No, they needed someone at the forefront of geology, a figurehead for British science. What was wanted was someone to fly the flag, so to speak.

What about Richard Owen, the famous anatomist? He was well known for his work on all sorts of fossils. He was certainly an important figure in scientific circles. William Clift, who sat on the committee and had employed Owen for many years, could vouch for his brilliance and reliability. His son-in-law had already eased up on the amount of work he did in his medical practice, so he wasn't under as much day-to-day pressure.

Richard Owen got the job. He was given a grant, which would help fund the travelling he had to do. If he was to gather together all the information that was then known about British fossil reptiles, he had to visit as many collections as possible. He began to compile his report.

Meanwhile, as if to illustrate his brilliance, Owen identified an unknown creature from just a fragment of bone, brought from New Zealand by a Dr John Rule. The piece he was shown was about 15 centimetres long and 14 centimetres in circumference at its narrowest point. It looked rather like a section of femur, or thigh bone, but with the rounded ends broken off. Owen at first thought it was the bone of an ox, but then noticed there were similarities to an ostrich femur. From that one broken section he announced that, in his opinion, this bone was from the thigh of a gigantic flightless bird. The bone wasn't fossilized, but Owen couldn't see how a bird that huge could strut around New Zealand without anyone noticing, so he pronounced it extinct. There was a lot of controversy over whether it really could be from a giant bird, but after more bones were sent to London four years later, he was proved right – and the moa, as it was known, actually turned out to be even bigger than an ostrich.

then the president of the Geological Society, praised his genius in recognizing the undreamed-of world that, it was now realized, had once existed. What particularly pleased Mantell, when the medal was presented, was the warm and enthusiastic reaction from the audience. He was accepted as an authority on fossil reptiles. This was what he had struggled for all these years.

So why the low spirits? It was probably a combination of the deteriorating relationship between him and Mary Ann, and the fact that there wasn't much money coming in. *"Very unhappy and unsettled,"* he wrote miserably. *"Alas! I have not found the path of peace."* He had let the medical practice slide while he focused so intently on building up a picture of the prehistoric world his *Iguanodon* might have inhabited.

Mantell's problems multiplied, with neuralgia, fever and delirium, and a mouth abscess, along with the usual colds and chills. But worst of all were the money problems. He hadn't been able to sell his old home, Castle Place in Lewes, so he'd had to put a tenant in. That brought in some cash, but the lump sum of a sale would have done much more good at a time like this.

The lack of patients was serious. Mantell was forced to stay indoors, just in case someone turned up needing medical attention. He couldn't afford to miss even one patient. He still remembered the time when he had been out gossiping with friends, then returned home to find a very important lady had sent for him to visit. Her servant had, of course, immediately gone to look for another doctor. Mantell didn't dare risk that happening again. But staying in, of course, meant he couldn't go to London to attend his regular meetings of the scientific societies, or those of the new BAAS. He was slowly slipping out of the public eye.

Sadly, Mantell needn't really have bothered to stay indoors waiting. Hardly anyone came. The situation began to get desperate – so desperate, in fact, that he gradually came to a shocking conclusion. He might have to do the unthinkable. He might have to sell his collection and buy a practice somewhere else.

Mantell's collection was his life. It was a tangible record of all he had done and all he had achieved. Without it, his scientific career would come to a total standstill.

He considered every option open to him. Going back to Lewes wasn't a possibility; his medical practice there had been sold and Castle Place was let. If it hadn't been for his rotten health – which he privately thought was caused by all his worries – Mantell might have settled Mary Ann and the children in a rented house and gone as ship's surgeon on an overseas expedition. Lecturing in America was another idea, but his favourite daughter, Hannah, was ill, and he couldn't bear to leave her. There was a drawback to everything he thought of. Selling the collection seemed to be the only way out. At least that would provide money to invest in a more thriving practice somewhere else.

Fortunately, Mantell had friends who were aware of the value of the collection, and they came up with an interesting suggestion. They proposed to start a scientific institution, right there in Brighton. They would open it to the public, who would pay an entry fee. The centrepiece of the institution – the main attraction – would be Gideon Mantell's fossil collection. If he would lend it to the institution, they said, they would pay him £250 a year.

This seemed a perfect scheme! And when the Earl of Egremont *"with his accustomed liberality"* donated another £1,000 to the venture, it seemed like the best thing for Mantell to do. But, as with all the other ideas for getting out of his financial difficulties, this one had its drawback. Unfortunately, it was a major one.

If Mantell was going to continue lecturing and looking after the few patients he had, then he must stay in Brighton. But the organizers of the institution wanted not only the collection, but the house, too. It was not a problem, they said. They could easily spare a small sitting room and bedroom for Mantell, but they would require the rest of the house. Of course, they'd pay him some rent – another £150 a year.

Mantell mentions few patients in his journal over the following months, and those seem to have been visited at home. It's likely that his small sitting room – his *"den"* – was unsuitable, being at the top of the tall, narrow house.

When she heard that she and her children, but not her husband, would have to leave their home, Mary Ann must have felt distraught, betrayed, but above all, angry. It's not surprising that on the last 25 December they spent together in their home, in 1835, Mantell wrote a single entry in his journal: *"One of the most miserable Xmas days I have ever spent."*

His relationship with Mary Ann worsened as the time drew near for the family to move out. On the day Mary Ann and the children moved to a rented cottage in Lewes, and Mantell moved to his own meagre rooms, he clearly didn't expect any great improvement in his circumstances. *"A change of circumstances with me is but a change of troubles,"* he wrote. His once lively family home was now silenced – given over to other men and prehistoric bones.

♪

The new Sussex Scientific Institution and Mantellian Museum was reasonably successful, although it needed a lot of advertising and promotion to keep the visitors coming. The big prize came a year after the opening of the institution, when the King and Queen granted it their patronage; from then on, it was known as the Sussex Royal Institution. But unlike the Earl of Egremont, the King and Queen didn't donate any money – the word "royal" had to do.

Gideon Mantell was giving extremely popular talks to the general public in the town hall, often to crowds of as many as 700 or 800. The bonus to him was that he managed to pick up a few patients along the way. Mary Ann had got over her initial rage and hurt and had moved to a cottage in Brighton, so Mantell was able to spend time with his family. His darling daughter Hannah, who had tuberculosis of the hip, even seemed better – for a while – although her illness gave Mantell a lot of heartache. His son, Walter, was apprenticed to a surgeon, just as Mantell had been. However, Walter was following in his father's footsteps in more ways than one – he was becoming keen on geology. To his delight, he'd even managed to find fossils that were new to his father. Walter added these to his own growing collection.

So, for a while, things were looking up. But during the following particularly foul winter, when Mantell was suffering from toothache and headaches, and overworked because everyone seemed to be going down with flu, his spirits plummeted again.

Mantell's dream was to get his family back together again, under one roof. It was clear that if he didn't, his marriage was doomed. But how? Getting regular patients for his practice was an uphill struggle. Perhaps people didn't fancy going to a doctor who was known to prefer spending his time fossil-collecting or chipping away at rocks. Whatever the reason for the lack of custom, there wasn't enough money coming in for him to even contemplate them all setting up home together again.

And so what if he *was* spending some of the little income he had on new fossils? Who could blame him? The collection was now the one stable thing in his life.

If only he'd known the BAAS had considered him for the "Report on British Fossil Reptiles". He could have told them the truth: he wasn't desperately busy with his medical practice – far from it. He would have welcomed the work, the grant and the prestige it would have brought him. One journal entry, when he'd been particularly down, read:

Could I but find a good professional opening (the more labour the better) and all would be well, and gracious Heaven would then reward me for all my past sufferings.

But it wasn't to be, and it soon became clear that the only way to resolve things was to move to where he could run a bigger practice, and so increase his income. But to buy a practice would take a substantial amount of money. Reluctantly, he came to the conclusion that there was no choice. This time the museum collection really would have to go.

It must have been an agonizing decision. The collection was part of Mantell's life – until recently, he would never, in his wildest dreams, have imagined it leaving his hands. The one thought he couldn't bear was that he might not get a buyer for the whole thing; it might have to be divided up and sold in smaller lots.

In desperation, Mantell offered it to the Sussex Royal Institution. Instead of paying him rent for it, would they be prepared to buy it outright? He asked for a first payment of £3,000 in cash – well below what it was worth – and said they could pay the balance over a period. He would accept £5,000 in total, he told them.

The Institution, as Mantell had probably suspected, didn't have the ready money to pay for the collection, so they decided to raise the cash by selling shares at £25 each. The Earl of Egremont, ever generous where Mantell was concerned, promised that when they'd sold a decent number of shares, he'd step in and buy a large block. He wanted to make sure the project was actually going to get off the ground before he invested any more money.

Having made his decision to sell, it must have been a slight consolation for Mantell to know the collection would stay in its present home. He would be able to visit it, examine pieces as he needed to, and watch people enjoying it.

In the meantime, he had to do something to ensure a good future income and a home for his family. Mantell decided to buy a medical practice in London, a going concern. After a bit of investigation, he found one that looked just right. It was at Clapham Common, which was a respectable suburb of London. As the practice was already established, the prospects were good. Mantell must have been cheered to be sure that at least one thing in his life was going to be all right. He would take over the new practice in the following spring, find a nice roomy house to rent, and move the family back in by late summer.

Then came a bitter blow. In November, 1837, the Earl of Egremont died. He still hadn't bought any shares, so now there was no hope that the Institution could raise all the money it needed. Therefore there was no hope that the Mantellian Museum might remain in Brighton.

It was going to cost Mantell a lot to buy the new practice and move to London. He'd been relying on the initial £3,000 from the sale of his fossils. Now there would be nothing. He was almost bankrupt. In the depths of despair, Mantell had to resign himself to the probability that the collection couldn't be sold as a whole but would have to be broken up and sold in bits.

Yet there was one final ray of light. After another desperately miserable Christmas, Mantell wrote to Charles König, Keeper of Geology at the British Museum, making an offer he hoped and prayed they couldn't refuse. *"The sum for which I offer my Museum to the National collection is £5,000 ... much less than I have expended in its formation,"* he wrote. He suggested they come and have a look at the collection to see its true value because, he added, putting a little spin on the offer, *"I am besieged with applications from local institutions"*.

The process of the British Museum officials deciding whether or not to buy the collection took time, and then deciding on the price took even longer. The whole collection had to be assessed and valued by a committee. William Buckland, paying Mantell a great compliment, suggested they should just pay the price he asked. Both the collection and Mantell were very well known to him – the collection was superb, and its owner, Buckland assured the committee members, was to be trusted.

While the British Museum people were dithering, Mantell took over the new medical practice at Clapham Common. Only the youngest child, Reginald, went with him. Walter was away studying, and Mary Ann and the two girls stayed behind in Brighton. Poor Hannah was still quite ill.

Eventually, a price of £4,000 was agreed for the sale of the whole Mantellian collection to the British Museum, and they would remove it from Brighton, they told him, just before Christmas.

There was one final condition: they didn't have the money to spare right now. Gideon Mantell couldn't have it until next August. This was yet another setback, but it was some compensation that the collection would be kept together. Mantell did at least know for sure that he would soon have a sum of money to help him out of his financial problems. Things had been pretty bad. But the family motto was *"Nil desperandum"*, and Mantell stuck by it. He didn't despair.

Owen
Reptile Report
1839–1841

IN AUGUST 1839, Richard Owen went to Birmingham where he was to be the centre of attention at a meeting of the BAAS. The focus of the meeting was Owen's "Report on British Fossil Reptiles".

On the day he set off for Birmingham, he woke from a rotten night with a bad headache. He felt terrible when he arrived and went to bed early. In fact, he was so unwell he was forced to miss an invitation to dinner at the home of Sir Robert Peel, the former Prime Minister. Owen was upset about that, but knew it was only sensible to rest, otherwise he wouldn't be fit enough to read his report. And that he was determined to do. After all, he wrote, *"what with abbreviations and railroad scribblings, nobody could read the MS* [manuscript] *but myself"*.

As it turned out, he had to postpone the reading for a

couple of days anyway. He then dosed himself up to make sure he'd have a voice.

The report was a huge success. Owen had gathered together all the information he could glean on the different species of marine lizards, such as the ichthyosaur – the "fish-lizard" – and the long-necked plesiosaur, both of which had been discovered by the Dorset fossil-collector, Mary Anning. Owen took the opportunity to take issue with the scientists who were suggesting that creatures might change and develop over the years – evolving from one type of being into another. Where was the evidence for that, he demanded? Transmutation – the changing of one creature into another – was nonsense, Owen maintained. As God had made beings, so they stayed.

And since Richard Owen was the most widely respected comparative anatomist of the time, people listened.

The report was so well received, so much admired, that the BAAS immediately offered Owen another grant to do a "Report on British Fossil Reptiles II". This time he would include the land reptiles: not just crocodiles, but the newly discovered giant lizard-types – the *Iguanodon*, *Megalosaurus*, *Hylaeosaurus*, and so on.

Straight away, Owen set about gathering all the information available on these creatures. There were collections to see in all parts of the country. The new railroads were a great boon to Owen, who was a big train fan. In a letter to his wife he seemed quite excited by it all', talking of *"the incessant yell-shriek of the steam-screamer"*. The time it saved, and the relative comfort, made such a difference to travel that Owen heartily recommended it to his friends.

As well as private collections, Owen visited the museums which were open to the public. He got slightly irritated to find that whenever he stopped to take notes about a fossil, a small crowd would gather round him, curious to see what he was doing. Nevertheless, if his report was to be thorough – and he was determined it would be – all this travelling and information-gathering had to be done. His report had to be bang up to date.

In Horsham, not far from Mantell's Tilgate Forest, Owen met a fossil collector called George Bax Holmes, who was quite happy to let the eminent Professor Owen borrow great chunks of his collection. And yes, of course, he could take them to London to study for his report.

Back in London, however, was the plum! Just a brisk walk away from Owen's home lay the British Museum. In the museum there was one very special collection. It was Gideon Mantell's life's work on fossil reptiles. Owen knew Mantell's reputation well. The two men met socially, not just at the scientific societies, and would often have discussed their interests. How Owen must have rubbed his hands together; the collection would yield a massive amount of material for his report. The fruits of Mantell's devotion to science lay waiting to be plucked, and used.

Fossil reptiles weren't the only thing on Owen's mind at this time. He seemed to have an unlimited capacity for work. He was shortly made president of the newly formed Microscopical Society – microscopes were the new big thing among scientists and Owen, of course, had one. At the first meeting of the society, his wife noted in her diary, Owen had to do a lot of speaking and was tired and starving hungry by the time he got home. Nevertheless, his day wasn't over yet. After he'd eaten, *"he sat up and finished the Plesiosaurus papers"*.

The year 1840 saw the publication of Owen's book, *Odontography*. This was the result of lots of studies of teeth, using the microscope. Owen worked so hard on this that he began to have eye trouble and reluctantly had to entrust some of the drawings to others.

In February of the same year, Owen was elected to the exclusive Athenaeum Club. Members were men distinguished in science, art and literature, and Professor Owen certainly fulfilled that requirement. In fact, he was becoming widely regarded as the British Cuvier – an accolade once bestowed by some scientists on Gideon Mantell, who was himself elected to the Athenaeum on the same day.

Owen would have been highly gratified that not only did membership of this club acknowledge his scientific achievements, it also brought social recognition.

Meanwhile, he continued to gather material for his second report. He would almost certainly have had discussions on the subject with Gideon Mantell. When

Owen had just acquired his brand new microscope, he even invited Mantell to dinner, along with William Buckland. After they'd eaten, Caroline noted, Owen *"entertained them to their heart's content with the microscope"*. And when Mantell attended Owen's lectures, such as the one on fossil remains at the Royal Institution, the two men must have had much to discuss afterwards. Mantell was so knowledgeable about Owen's latest interest – the fossil land reptiles – that it's hard to believe Owen didn't pick his brains to acquire every scrap of information he could. And Mantell, being so passionate about his subject, would have talked enthusiastically and freely.

By August 1841, Owen's "Report on British Fossil Reptiles II" was ready. It was to be presented to the BAAS at Plymouth, in Devon. This was a much more relaxing affair for him than the one at Birmingham. He and Caroline went by boat from Southampton to Plymouth, and stayed with old friends.

Owen spoke for two and a half hours. He went into intricate detail on every known species of fossil reptile, which he divided into groups or families: one for the flying lizards, one for the crocodile types, and so on. One particular group he called Lacertians. These were the huge land lizards – the *Megalosaurus*, *Iguanodon*, and *Hylaeosaurus*. The man who named the first, Professor Buckland, was there listening to him. The man who'd discovered and named both the others, Gideon Mantell, wasn't.

These Lacertians, Owen claimed, were created by God. The ideas being put about – that they might have evolved from some other being – were complete rubbish, he claimed. The Reverend Professor Buckland, of course, was delighted to hear this being pronounced by such an eminent scientist, but not everybody would have been in agreement. Evidence was slowly being gathered that appeared to show that animal life did indeed change over long periods of time. However, Buckland swept that from his mind and, as soon as the report was finished, he stood up and complimented Professor Owen on his hard work, and on how the audience had been riveted by what he had to say.

Owen himself was extremely satisfied with the response, both from the audience and the BAAS. He was immediately offered yet another grant, of £200, if he'd produce a third report. Things just got better and better.

"My Sweet Girl..."

1839–1841

IN THE SPRING OF 1839, Mary Ann Mantell came to a decision. Sick of all the rows, the worries and the separations, she had had enough. The marriage, she clearly felt, was beyond saving, and there was no way on this earth she was going to go and live in London. Mary Ann took the unusual and courageous (for the times) step of leaving her husband completely. She and her housekeeper went to live in a cottage near Exeter, in the west of England.

Their elder son, Walter, added to Mantell's hurt and misery by announcing he wasn't going to follow in his father's footsteps. It had always been assumed that he would set up as a doctor in his own medical practice, or maybe go into partnership with his father. But it wasn't to be. Walter had decided to emigrate to New Zealand. This was a dreadful prospect for Mantell. A young man emigrating to the other side of the world in the mid-1800s was unlikely ever to see his family again.

An extra twist of the knife was Mantell's daughter Ellen's decision to leave home to live with a friend and attend school in south-east London. With Reginald away at school, too, Mantell was left with just his beloved Hannah. Although she had to spend all her time in bed, she was still able to read, sew, draw and paint. However, she was very ill, needing constant care. *"My poor child continues to suffer on, without any prospect of recovery."* Mantell himself was having fainting spells, and still had attacks of agonizing facial neuralgia. In fact, he confided to a friend, *"I have been suffering deeply of late in both mind and body."*

There was worse to come. In February 1840, along with Richard Owen, Mantell had been elected to the Athenaeum. It was a great honour to become a member, and he was very flattered and uplifted by it. But on the first evening at his new club, Mantell suddenly became agitated about Hannah. Although there were servants in the house, he had never left her unless he was visiting a patient, until that night. He hurried home.

Within a few minutes of her father's arrival, Hannah was bleeding severely from an open wound on her diseased hip. She fainted, and remained very weak for the next few days. Mantell was frantic with worry. This was his most beloved child; he adored her.

Hannah's aunt and cousin were sent for, so someone could be with her constantly. Now she need never be left alone for a second.

On 12 March, Hannah suddenly felt very ill indeed. Her father was in a room nearby, and she asked her cousin to call him. She was bleeding badly again. Soon she was unconscious, slipping away. Within a few minutes, she died. She was only 17.

Five days later, at West Norwood Cemetery in south London, Mantell buried Hannah, the daughter he'd so loved and whose gentleness and affection had meant so much to him. *"My sweet girl, Hannah Matilda..."* the broken-hearted father wrote in his journal, *"one whose sweetness of disposition, and affectionate heart endeared her to me beyond even the natural ties that united us, is taken from me!"* Mantell's misery and depression were almost too great for him to bear.

Mantell's books were selling well. At the Royal Society he was even introduced to Prince Albert, the new young husband of Queen Victoria (William IV's successor), and was able to present him with a copy of his latest book, *The Wonders of Geology*. People who knew about such things forecast that this book was going to bring Gideon Mantell great success. He'd written it for a more general readership, so it would be easy for all to understand, and Charles Lyell reckoned it would go a long way towards making science popular. People would be eager to know more about the newly discovered monsters.

The book didn't bring Mantell huge amounts of money, but it did sell steadily for many years. He was pleased with its reception, saying, *"my farewell to geology has ... been a flattering finale to my labours"*. He clearly wasn't expecting, at that time, to resume his scientific career.

And, of course, there was the exhibiting of his collection at the British Museum. It would be gratifying to see it displayed in such a great and grand institution for the whole world to see. But when Mantell went to see it four months after Hannah's death, he was extremely disappointed to find only part of it was on show – just the bones of the *Iguanodon* and *Hylaeosaurus*. *"All the rest still under cover!!! It is too bad,"* he wrote.

At the beginning of 1841 Gideon Mantell felt he'd got himself back into some sort of balance, but was clearly lonely. *"Alas!"* he wrote, *"I have no home for my affections."* He settled into life as a doctor once more, but continued writing, contributing occasional papers to the Royal Society. He generally didn't read his own papers at meetings, but on at least one occasion, he must have wished he had when, he complained, it *"was read, or rather mumbled, and mutilated"*. All that work, and half the audience probably didn't hear it.

One day in August, Mantell picked up his copy of the *Literary Gazette*. There was a report of Professor Richard Owen's talk to the BAAS in Plymouth on fossil reptiles. Mantell read it, first with interest, and then with growing disbelief. Owen spoke as if he was correcting

Mantell's mistaken conclusions about the *Iguanodon* and the *Hylaeosaurus*. Mantell was indignant. The man should have made it clear he was actually building on work that he – Mantell – had already done! The discoveries Owen had made about Mantell's fossil reptiles were the next steps in understanding them, so he should have been acknowledging the solid groundwork already laid before he even became involved with them.

As Mantell pointed out in a letter to a friend, Owen appeared to have forgotten that when he, Mantell, had written those papers, he was a pioneer in the science of fossil reptiles – he *"did not possess the advantage of former labourers"* as Owen had done. The use of microscopes had given Owen an advantage Mantell had never had. For instance, Owen had examined *Iguanodon* teeth and those of the modern iguana microscopically, and announced in his report that there was no great similarity. As far as Professor Richard Owen was concerned, the extinct *Iguanodon* was the *Iguanodon* and the living iguana was the iguana. How could there be any relationship between them? He managed to make Mantell look a fool for assuming there was any relationship and pointed out that, consequently, even the name *Iguanodon* – "iguana tooth" – had been a mistake.

Mantell was seething with anger. He immediately wrote a letter to the *Literary Gazette* defending himself. He'd discovered the *Iguanodon*, and had virtually built up a picture of the whole animal from just a few bones. Working without a microscope, he'd compared the teeth of the *Iguanodon* and the iguana and seen that they were similar except, of course, in size. He continued, doing his best to defend himself. The letter was courteous, but made it clear that Owen had given the impression that he was responsible for work which had actually been done by Mantell, who now demanded credit where credit was due. Mantell thought this behaviour was totally unworthy of a renowned scientist; he felt his work had been almost stolen from him – and by a man who had probably never set foot in a quarry in his life, much less found a bone for himself!

Maybe it was this incident which spurred Mantell on to start building another collection. He certainly wasn't going to let Owen walk all over him. He was fired up now. So, while Owen busied himself in preparing his report and drawings for publication, Mantell was also out and about. He visited quarries, searching for more fossils, and got in touch again with people like Bensted, who had supplied him with the "Mantell-piece". He planned a new paper to present to the Royal Society. In it, Mantell was going to include his latest thinking about what the *Iguanodon* actually looked like and how it behaved. He'd decided that he'd rather over-estimated the size. The *Iguanodon* was probably smaller than he'd thought at first. Nevertheless, it was still a colossal beast. He also had particular new theories about its front legs. This was going to make people sit up and realize that Gideon Mantell was still very much a force to be reckoned with in the geological world.

And then, one October day in 1841, everything changed. Mantell was riding in his carriage – his chariot, as he called it – when the coachman completely lost control and the reins became tangled. Recklessly, Mantell tried to grab the reins himself in an attempt to stop the horse. The combination of his precarious position and the bouncing, jolting carriage meant he was thrown out. He crashed to the ground, and was dragged along, probably because he was still clinging to the reins.

Although the wheels grazed Mantell's head, mercifully they didn't run over him, and he wrote in his journal, no doubt with great relief, that he'd *"narrowly escaped severe injury"*.

He was wrong. He soon fell victim to symptoms of numbness in his lower limbs, commenting two or three weeks later that it was so bad that he could barely walk. Paralysis was setting in. He suffered from cramps, and soon found the numbness had spread to his right arm.

Mantell's final journal entry for the year records how, although the paralysis was somewhat improved, he couldn't walk without help: *"I terminate this year in a state of great bodily suffering."*

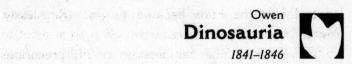

Owen
Dinosauria
1841–1846

WHILE MANTELL'S PLANS to publish his new theory about the *Iguanodon*'s front legs were put on hold because of his prolonged illness, Richard Owen was also coming to some conclusions about legs. He reckoned he was about to prove that Gideon Mantell had made a big mistake.

Having applied his anatomist's skills to fossilized leg bones, Owen was beginning to wonder if, instead of these giant lizards having legs which sprawled out to the side as a modern crocodile's do, their legs were held below the body, supporting it from beneath like an elephant's. Perhaps they didn't crawl along like a crocodile, low to the ground. Perhaps they walked high, on sturdy legs, like a mammal. But how could a reptile's simple spine carry the enormous weight of those huge bodies?

Owen continued working on the ancient fossil reptiles as he prepared his report for publication, and the more he studied them, the more fascinated he became. There weren't many people working on them. Perhaps he saw a chance for advancement here.

Then Owen heard that George Bax Holmes, the Horsham collector who'd proved so helpful in the past, had found some *Iguanodon* bones. They were, Holmes assured him, even bigger than those Mantell had found.

Owen knew that Mantell had estimated the size of his *Iguanodon* by comparing it with the creature it most closely resembled – the modern iguana – and scaling it up accordingly. But now, when he looked at this new, larger bone and applied the same system, he came up with a creature approaching 60 metres in length. It just wouldn't wash. Something that big would have bones so huge and heavy it wouldn't be able to move. He was convinced Mantell was wrong, and set out to prove it.

The method Owen developed to work out the size of the reptiles was by measuring the vertebrae and estimating how many bones there were in the spine. Using this technique, he calculated that the *Iguanodon* was only about eight or nine metres long, just over a third as long as Mantell's most recent guess.

Although Owen behaved in a perfectly proper way to Mantell whenever they met socially, it's unlikely that he felt anything remotely like friendship for him. Mantell was constantly making new discoveries, which rather put him in the limelight. Now Owen, with his new method for calculating the size of the *Iguanodon*, could push its discoverer into the shadows. In his next big report, he would prove that Mantell was wrong!

William Saull, the man who had accompanied Mantell to Maidstone to see the "Mantell-piece", had bought a new *Iguanodon* fossil, which had been found on the Isle of Wight. It was a section of the lower spine called the sacrum. It's fairly certain Saull would have let Mantell know of this new fossil, but Mantell was still barely able to walk without severe pain, and didn't feel up to travelling across London. Richard Owen was the first to see it.

As he made his way through the London streets to see Saull, Owen had no idea that what he was about to see would give him a vital clue which, coupled with his brilliance as an anatomist, would make him famous even outside scientific circles; more famous than Cuvier – or Gideon Mantell.

Meanwhile Owen had been busy preparing his second "Report on British Fossil Reptiles" for publication. Of course, there would be a certain amount of rewriting, as text in a published paper is more formal than the spoken word. Mistakes would be corrected. But it was not usual for talks to be substantially changed between the public reading and publication. There were also many scientific drawings to be prepared. That wasn't a problem as the association had given him £250 to pay for them. But they would take quite a time to complete.

Richard Owen needed that time. He urgently wanted to make some alterations to his talk before publication, and the alterations would be substantial. Maybe it was a mark of his importance and power that he was able to make such changes and get away with it. But when he'd started rewriting his report, little did he know he was going to be making an even bigger, more dramatic change.

The *Iguanodon* sacrum Saull had bought was made up of five vertebrae. They were different from the vertebrae which had already been discovered, in that they were fused together. This wasn't new: Owen had seen that Buckland's *Megalosaurus* had part of its lower spine fused. But he now realized that he had the final clue to the mystery of the legs!

The fused sacrum – the rigid set of vertebrae – would make the whole backbone much stronger than had previously been thought. In mammals, the sacrum forms the strongest part of the hip or pelvis. Coupled with his ideas about legs, this would change the way everybody visualized the beasts. All those drawings of low-slung, sprawled lizards could go out of the window, as far as he was concerned. Everyone would have to think differently, thanks to him.

Owen knew the sea lizards, such as the plesiosaur and ichthyosaur, didn't have a fused sacrum. Was this because they didn't need the extra strength? Because water

*Gideon Mantell, who discovered the fossilized teeth and bones of the
Iguanodon in a Sussex quarry.*

Richard Owen holds a bone from the leg of the extinct giant flightless bird from New Zealand: the moa.

Mary Ann Mantell, who found a fossilized tooth in 1822 that marked a significant step in the discovery of dinosaurs.

Worn Iguanodon *teeth found by Gideon and Mary Ann Mantell. (The tooth on the right is 5.3 cm long.)*

The Hunterian Museum at the Royal College of Surgeons in London,
where Richard Owen worked for nearly 30 years

A dinner party inside the mould of the Crystal Palace Iguanodon. Richard Owen is at the head of the table (inside the head of the Iguanodon).

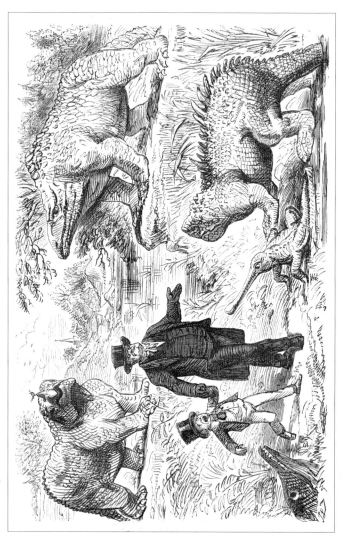

A Victorian boy gets his first glimpse of a prehistoric world in the grounds of the Crystal Palace.

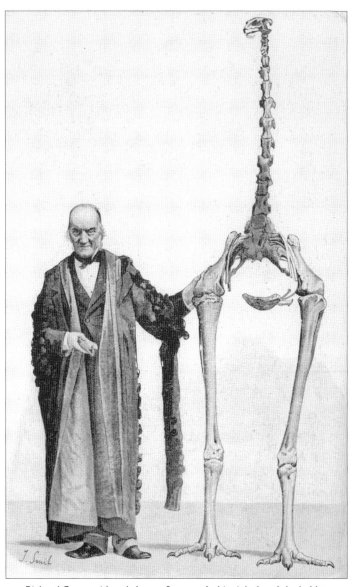

Richard Owen with a skeleton of a moa. In his right hand, he holds a fragment of the femur.

By the time these skeletons were reconstructed, following their discovery in 1878, scientists believed that the Iguanodon walked on two legs, trailing its tail. It's now known that it probably walked both on two legs and on all fours, and used its tail as a counterbalance.

supported their big bodies? And the flying lizards – the pterosaurs – they didn't have a fused sacrum. With their light bones, they also wouldn't have needed the extra strength it would have given.

But if the lizards like *Megalosaurus* and *Iguanodon* that lived on land were as gigantic as it seemed, they had an awful lot of body and tail to support. The fused sacrum, together with the strong, straight, elephant-like legs he believed they had, would give them the support and strength they needed simply to move around.

Megalosaurus was a carnivore. *Iguanodon* was a herbivore. They were both huge; both reptiles. Both had a fused sacrum, similar to the one mammals have. Both had straight legs beneath their bodies, as only Richard Owen had realized. It dawned on him that these characteristics set the gigantic land reptiles apart from the marine and flying reptiles, and put them in a class of their own – *"a distinct tribe"*.

A distinct tribe would need a name of its own. Owen pondered. He wanted to think of something simple, direct and memorable which would suit these colossal creatures.

By the time his report was finally published in April 1842, Owen had a name. *"The combination of such characters..."*, he wrote, *"...will, it is presumed, be deemed sufficient ground for establishing a distinct tribe or suborder of Saurian Reptiles for which I would propose the name of Dinosauria."* Richard Owen had used two Greek words to coin the name dinosaur: *"deinos"*, which means "terrible", and *"sauros"*, which means "lizard". He went on to talk of the most remarkable examples of his new tribe as being *"the Megalosaurus, Iguanodon, and Hylaeosaurus, the worthy fruits of the laborious researches of Professor Buckland and Dr Mantell"*.

In publishing the report, and naming the huge beasts, Owen had appropriated the dinosaurs from all those who'd done so much work on them: men like Buckland, who'd spent so much time working on the *Megalosaurus* fossils; and, of course, Gideon Mantell, who had been the one to fight to bring to light the very existence of giant prehistoric reptiles, and who had visualized the world they lived in. Owen had defined *Megalosaurus*, *Iguanodon* and *Hylaeosaurus* as a group that stood alone. He had given them their name – the terrible lizards. And by naming them, he had taken them for his own. Dinosaurs were his, and he hoped that they would be remembered as his.

Nothing seemed to touch Richard Owen. He was unstoppable and utterly sure of himself. He would have known Mantell was ill and didn't have the energy to fight him in public. And Mantell's complaints in the *Literary Gazette* about Owen's behaviour when he made his report at Plymouth hadn't harmed his reputation a bit.

Owen's power base grew when he was appointed joint conservator at the Hunterian Museum, alongside his ex-boss, William Clift. Among other activities, he was working on the next report for the BAAS, this time on fossil mammals, and had almost finished the second volume of *Odontography*, his huge undertaking on the comparative anatomy of teeth.

Owen's success, if not his methods of achieving it, was noticed in high places. One November day, he went into work and found an official-looking letter. It was from the Prime Minister, Sir Robert Peel, who was now back in office for a second time. To Owen's delight, he read that Peel had recommended to Queen Victoria that he, Professor Richard Owen, should be given a pension from the civil list. This was an amount of money set aside by Parliament to pay the expenses of the Queen and her household. With the advice of her ministers, some of it could be used to grant pensions to people who were distinguished in the arts or sciences. It's a mark of how highly the Prime Minister regarded Owen that the amount offered was £200. Not a great sum in itself, but it was about two thirds of the whole amount Peel had at his disposal. The pension was *"to encourage that devotion to science for which you are so eminently distinguished"*. Caroline Owen told how her husband wasted no time in putting on his boots and hurrying to a friend who helped him compose a letter accepting the pension. A month or so later, Peel asked to see the Hunterian Museum and spent two hours there while Owen identified the various fossils for him.

It was shortly after this that a box of fossils from New Zealand was sent to Professor Buckland. In it were some bones which appeared to belong to the creature Richard

Owen had identified four years before as a giant, flightless bird, the moa. Buckland sent the box on to him.

Examination of these new finds proved to Owen that he'd been absolutely right. It was a bird, far too heavy to fly, and it certainly was a giant: the moa stood about three and a half metres high – a metre taller than an ostrich. Owen's already brilliant reputation blossomed further when the news got around, even attracting the attention of Prince Albert.

Owen's social star certainly had risen, and he frequently mixed with the celebrities of the day: statesmen, foreign royalty, writers and artists. Owen also met the celebrated author, Charles Dickens, whose books he loved.

Dinosaurs were so talked-about now, not just in Britain, but in Europe and America, too, that Dickens introduced them into the very first paragraph of one of his books, *Bleak House*. Describing a filthy November day, he told how the London streets were so foul and muddy that they were like the aftermath of the Great Flood.

As much mud in the streets, as if the waters had but newly retired from the face of the earth, and it would not be wonderful to meet a Megalosaurus, forty feet long or so, waddling like an elephantine lizard up Holborn Hill.

Dickens even mentioned the famous dinosaur professor in another novel, *Our Mutual Friend*, when a character called

Mrs Podsnap was reflected in a mirror and described as being a *"fine woman for Professor Owen, quantity of bone, neck and nostrils like a rocking-horse, hard features..."*. Clearly Mrs Podsnap had a dinosaurian appearance!

Sir Robert Peel paid Owen the great compliment of commissioning a portrait of him, to be hung alongside that of Georges Cuvier. Peel checked first with Buckland that Owen, who was such a busy man, would be happy to spare the time to sit for an artist. He would! This must have given Owen enormous satisfaction – the great French Cuvier, and the great "British Cuvier", one each side of the entrance to Peel's gallery at his home, Drayton Manor.

Owen was indeed busy. One summer he had such a hectic schedule that he sent his wife and son, Willie, on holiday by themselves to Dover. He made time, when he could, to pay them a visit for a few days, and then went straight back to work. Over this period, Owen also found time to read a book which had been sent to him and which, at first, intrigued him. It was intriguing because it had been written anonymously. The title was *Vestiges of the Natural History of Creation*, and Owen wasn't the only one to be profoundly disturbed by what he read – a friend told him he thought it was a *"beastly book"*. *Vestiges* argued the case for evolution. The author, a journalist named Robert Chambers, tried to prove it was not true that animals had been created and then stayed in exactly the same form until the species died out. He believed there was steady change over vast periods of time, one species gradually developing and evolving into something different.

In normal circumstances, Owen would have written a review of the book that would have consigned it to oblivion. However, for once he kept quiet, because he was beginning to change his own views somewhat. In fact he was developing his own theory, according to which all vertebrate creatures were based on, and had developed from, an original archetype – a blueprint – created by God.

Meanwhile, Owen had excelled himself again, and his work had reaped a fresh honour. He'd produced a paper for the Royal Society on the belemnite – an extinct mollusc from the same family as the squid and octopus. Its bullet-shaped fossil is part of its internal shell, at the opposite end to its tentacles. Owen named this fossil after himself, calling it *Belemnites owenii*, and described it according to his findings. People were impressed; yet another discovery by the great Professor Owen, the top anatomist of his time! And in 1846, for this work, the Royal Society presented him with the coveted Royal Medal.

Slights and Insults
1842–1847

MANTELL CONTINUED TO SUFFER long after his carriage accident. He took hot baths to try to relieve some of the symptoms, but they left him so exhausted that he had to give up. When he was worn out from exerting himself, the numbness became worse, and he wasn't able to walk. By his fifty-second birthday in February, he must have been very much weakened, both physically and mentally, by what he called *"my long and serious illness"*.

But on his birthday Mantell received a great compliment and the early promise of a wonderful gift. The rector from his church and many of the local people had clubbed together to buy Dr Mantell, *"who is one of the most persevering and successful cultivators of science in this country"*, a microscope. It was a gesture of thanks and respect for his excellent lectures, and for promoting scientific knowledge in the neighbourhood. His talks and drawings of dinosaurs had fired the imaginations of people who had known nothing of geology before they went to listen to the doctor. Now they were telling their friends to come and hear about the amazing buried world of the dinosaurs.

The microscope was a wonderful gift for Mantell, and when he received it, and the apparatus which went with it, he was thrilled to find it was one of the very best available. It was inscribed to him from his friends in the neighbourhood as being *"in testimony of their grateful sense of his kind and effective exertions among them for the advancement of scientific knowledge"*.

Maybe the gift gave a much-needed boost to his spirits for, although still suffering, Mantell began to get out and about a little more, attending the odd lecture or exhibition, and continued to work on his latest book.

Around this time, Professor Owen's second "Report on British Fossil Reptiles" – the new, improved version – was published. Mantell was generous in calling it masterly, but furiously indignant at how Owen had made a point of highlighting any mistake Mantell had made. He had pointed out Mantell's errors in calculating the size of the *Iguanodon*, quoting his new estimates. This infuriated Mantell, who thought it grossly unfair, as he had revised his own estimates and announced this in a paper he'd read to the Royal Society at the beginning of the previous year – 15 months ago. Owen had conveniently ignored that.

All these slights and veiled insults seemed unnecessary and appallingly unjust to Mantell – after all, he'd been a pioneer in the discovery of dinosaurs. Owen had the full benefit of all his work and experience. Owen, Mantell wrote, exhibited *"a want of honour and I may say justice, towards those but for whose labour and zeal he could never have obtained the materials for his own reputation"*. He had written about Mantell's own fossils, which had already been scientifically described, as if they were his own discoveries. Owen, Mantell maintained, had talked of conclusions drawn *"as if originating with himself, when I had long since published the same"*.

Mantell couldn't understand why Owen wanted, or needed, to steal his thunder. And others agreed. Every item Owen had examined, every paper he'd read, had been the result of the work of those who'd been out there digging in quarries, seeking, collecting and studying fossils. A friend wrote to Mantell, saying Owen's treatment of him was *"unjust and dishonourable and merits exposure although it might not be wise"*. This seems to suggest the friend thought Owen would make a dangerous enemy.

In spite of Owen's report, Mantell was feeling considerably better as spring wore on. The numbness had almost left his legs, although it could be easily brought on again if he overdid things. He still had neuralgia in his face and felt, as he put it, *"greatly debilitated"*, but managed to give a lecture to a crowded room at the London Institution. Dinosaur-talk was spreading. There were often news items and drawings of incredible creatures in the papers, and people couldn't get enough of them. Mantell was pleased to meet many of his friends that evening, and even more pleased to be enthusiastically clapped at the end.

In late April, Mantell attended a lecture given by Owen, and had the pleasure – and no doubt surprise – of hearing the professor hold him up as an example to the listening students. Dr Mantell, he said, had shown it was perfectly possible to research a scientific subject while running an *"extensive, active and successful practice"*.

It seems odd that Mantell could bring himself to face the man after Owen's *"unworthy piracy"* and insulting behaviour. Maybe a clue can be found in a passage of a letter he wrote shortly afterwards. He was telling his friend that Owen had been attacked several times by other scientists in the magazine *The Lancet* for his bad behaviour towards them. Mantell said he felt Owen had been through enough without him joining in, too.

My feelings are so subdued by my illness that I am more than ever anxious to live in charity with all men.

He later wrote that if his life were spared, and he had enough strength, he wanted to write a history of what he referred to as the country of the *Iguanodon*, detailing every aspect of life then that he could deduce from the Tilgate Forest remains. And then, he warned, *"I will defend the rights and assert my claims."* But at the time, he was feeling so bad that he suspected he might not live long and it would be up to his son, Reginald, to defend his father's honour. He was, when he could manage it, sorting out his papers so everything would be left in proper order.

◀

After Owen's lecture, Mantell had the honour of entertaining Prince Albert at a prestigious soirée. He'd taken his microscope with him to show the scientists present some interesting examples of pond life. As soon as the Prince arrived, he was taken straight to Mantell, and became extremely interested in the microscope. He used it for more than half an hour, which pleased its owner no end. But the excitement was too much for Mantell. He returned home totally worn out.

Over the next few weeks, Mantell was occasionally confined to bed with terrible pain. He was taking a mixture of a dilute solution of opium, called laudanum, together with prussic acid, to try to get relief. He did his best to carry on as near normal a life as possible. After all, he had to earn money to survive. When he did take a short break, he visited Charles Lyell and his wife. They were pleased to see him, but quite taken aback by Mantell's appearance which, to them, seemed ghastly. Pain and suffering were taking their toll. Even when the pain did ease, Mantell had difficulty sleeping, finding no peace of mind. He spent much of the small hours reading, *"to keep my thoughts silent"*.

In June he visited the British Museum with Reginald and his daughter, Ellen, no doubt eager to see his specimens displayed. He was truly angry to find one of his own *Hylaeosaurus* bones on the floor, broken. He picked up the bits and handed them to an attendant. In Mantell's opinion, this important collection, which belonged to the nation, was being badly neglected. On a more personal level, *"This bone is unique,"* he wrote, *"and cost me several nights' labour to extricate it from the stone!"* Ten days later he was back again, and took it upon himself to rearrange some of the *Iguanodon* specimens. It was hurtful to see something over which he'd lavished such care, and which was so important to modern science, treated as if it was no more than a piece of common pottery.

In August, even though one thigh and foot were numb again, and he had severe back pain when he stood or walked, Mantell left on a trip by rail to Bristol and Wales, and was able to enjoy a good deal of it. Whatever part of the country he went to, there were always collections to see and fresh specimens to collect. He managed some sightseeing, too, but when he returned he began to suffer from sciatica, which gave him excruciating pain in the lower part of his back and down his leg. On one occasion he recorded having 20 leeches placed on his body to suck out his blood in an attempt to give him some relief.

By September, Mantell found something worrying.

A tumour of considerable size has gradually made its appearance on the left side of the spine ... probably a lumbar abscess; and my long probation of suffering

will be terminated by a painful and lingering death.
Well – be it so...

The many doctors he consulted couldn't agree on what the lump was, and neither could they agree on the treatment. In terrible pain for an average of 15 hours out of 24, he ended the year *"in a state of great suffering"*.

For the first few months of 1843, Gideon Mantell was very unwell. He was now suffering from an added complication: a hugely swollen leg. His doctors decided that the lump on his back was an abscess. They recommended he stay lying down, and keep perfectly quiet. The next entry in his journal says he went to a lecture by Charles Lyell, so he clearly didn't agree with the diagnosis. Secretly, he was convinced it was cancer.

Mantell wasn't, of course, able to do anything practical in the way of fossil collecting, but he did manage to begin a new book. He pushed himself into working regularly on the manuscript, but wrote, *"It is very irksome to write while writhing in severe pain."* He managed to overcome this to a certain extent, by training himself to write while lying down. After a rotten Christmas, Mantell sent the first part of his new book to the publisher. The full manuscript – a thousand pages – was finally finished in May 1844, and was published in two volumes. This was an extraordinary achievement in view of his almost constant suffering.

Throughout all this time, Mantell continued to try to build up his second fossil collection, acquiring specimens from wherever and whomever he could, and working on them as he was able to. He still had patients to see, but because of his own health problems, his medical practice was running down. He just wasn't able to keep up the pace. The lease on his house was due to run out, so another move was soon on the cards. This time he chose to move closer to the heart of London, to a much smarter area. He leased a tall, narrow, but elegant house in Chester Square, not far from Buckingham Palace, for 21 years, with an option to end the lease after five years if he wished. He wrote, quite candidly, that he expected five years was all he'd need.

By the end of September, the Mantell household had settled into Chester Square. Although most of the family had now left, there was still quite a sizeable number of people for one man to support. His sister and younger son, Reginald, who was now apprenticed to the engineer Isambard Kingdom Brunel, still lived with him. There were three servants to feed and pay, plus an assistant. He also sent money to Mary Ann, and to his daughter Ellen, who was planning to marry a publisher. He'd even been sending money to his brother, *"poor Joshua"*, who was disabled and lived in an institution.

Mantell's plan now was to earn an income by giving lectures – he already had six booked – and by travelling back and forth between Chester Square and Clapham to treat what patients he still had left.

It's possible that moving somewhere new, even with all the effort and planning involved, bucked up his spirits, because in October 1844 Mantell wrote, *"General state of health rather better; attacks of neuralgia much less severe."* By the next Christmas, which he described as *"cheerless"*, the suspected tumour had stopped growing, the sciatica had eased considerably and he was able to walk at least three miles at a time, although painfully. Things didn't seem to have got any worse, but the whole year, he concluded, hadn't got any better as it went along, and money was a constant niggling worry.

Then Mantell's publisher suggested he write a book about the geology of the Isle of Wight. The island had already proved to be a great hunting ground for dinosaur fossils, and now it had the added attraction of royal approval. The young Queen Victoria, still in her mid-twenties, wasn't madly keen on Brighton. She and Prince Albert had bought Osborne House on the Isle of Wight. Where royalty went, the aristocracy followed, and suddenly the island was the place to be. The book should therefore be a good seller, and Mantell set himself a deadline. He wanted it to be ready to sell at the next BAAS meeting in Southampton. He managed to get a bit of extra publicity, and attracted royal attention into the bargain, when he took a geological model of the Isle of Wight to one of Lord Northampton's soirées. Prince Albert spent ages chatting to Mantell about it. When the book, *Geological Excursions Round the Isle of Wight*, was eventually finished, Mantell dedicated it to the prince.

As he wrote, Mantell was gradually drawing together his conclusions – arrived at from years of research – about the *Iguanodon*. He knew the length was being estimated in different ways, and that they couldn't all be right. Now he was coming round to Owen's estimation of about eight or nine metres. Mantell pictured a body the size of a large elephant, with thick strong legs at the back, smaller, lighter front legs, and a single horn on the nose. The fossil horn was something like the horn on a particular species of iguana, and Mantell was particularly satisfied by this extra likeness between the modern and the ancient creatures. Consequently, he was sure it would have sat on the *Iguanodon*'s nose. The horn was, he wrote, *"equal in size, and not very different in form, to the lesser horn of the rhinoceros"*. There was no question that the beast was herbivorous – the teeth indicated that. Its jaws were powerful, and able to cope with the very tough vegetation Mantell believed it would have eaten.

In November 1846, Mantell had been to a special anniversary meeting of the Royal Society. Among the awards being presented that evening was the Royal Medal. Mantell watched in disbelief as the medal was presented to Professor Richard Owen for his paper on belemnites. It's likely Mantell knew Owen was in the chair at the meeting when his paper was proposed for the medal, so perhaps he felt a little suspicious that all was not above board. However, Owen would certainly have suggested to the other members present that he felt a bit awkward about chairing a discussion of his own work, so he would have left the room while it was proposed again – and granted.

The reason for Mantell being so staggered that Owen had got the Royal Medal was that he was convinced the belemnite paper had been full of mistakes. Mantell knew a thing or two about belemnites, and remembered a paper, by a man called Pearce, which had been read before the Geological Society a few years previously. Owen had been at that meeting, and had heard Pearce describe a group of fossils – a genus – which he named *Belemnoteuthis*. Pearce stated that some fossils which people mistakenly called belemnites really belonged to the *Belemnoteuthis* genus. Owen had made that mistake. He had also made the mistake of making no reference in his own paper to Pearce's work, which is unacceptable behaviour in scientific circles.

Mantell went home and recorded the event in his journal. He was appalled at this *"paper which turns out unfortunately to be a tissue of blunders from beginning to end! So much for Medalism."*

Not long afterwards, Mantell received a package from his younger son. Reginald was now working on the Great Western Railway in Wiltshire, with Brunel. To his father's intense pride, Reginald had proved himself so good at his work that Brunel had cancelled the apprenticeship and was now employing him and paying him a proper wage. Reginald paid close attention as new ground was excavated, and sometimes sent his father interesting fossil finds.

When Mantell opened this particular package, he found the contents to be even more interesting than usual. It contained some magnificent examples of fossilized belemnites. Mantell began to examine them, very carefully. What he found seemed to provide the proof he needed that Owen's paper on belemnites was based on error. It was time to write a paper of his own.

Meanwhile, another box arrived, just before Christmas. It was from Mantell's elder son, Walter, in New Zealand. Walter had given him a lot of extra worry, because he hadn't made much success of his new life. Mantell had sent him large sums of money to help him survive but things still went badly. However, Walter had never lost his interest in geology. He'd collected more than 800 fossils, and sent them to England. Among them were many moa bones. Mantell knew Richard Owen would be keen to see these. After all, they were a great interest of his.

It's difficult to understand why Mantell decided to let Owen examine the bones. Owen certainly knew far more about the bird than he did, but with some concentrated work, Mantell could have put that right. Perhaps he felt that the moa was rightfully Owen's discovery, so he should continue the work on it. He might have hoped that his generous gesture in handing the bones over would make Owen less hostile towards him, especially as he was about to write a paper negating some of Owen's claims about the belemnites. Whatever his reason, Mantell sat down and wrote a letter inviting Owen to come and see some fossils that would greatly interest him.

A Withering Attack

1847–1848

OWEN TOOK ONE LOOK at the moa bones and knew Walter had sent some unique specimens. No scientist had ever seen a moa jaw before, only skull fragments. Now, before him, was a perfect skull, complete with jaw. This would yield so much information about the giant bird and its habits. There were even eggshells!

Owen must have been ecstatic when Mantell offered the bones to him to make of them what he would. He was probably slightly surprised, too, and might have wondered why Mantell was being so generous, when the two of them didn't exactly get on. But Owen was well aware of the power he wielded in Britain's scientific world, and might have guessed Mantell would rather be on his good side.

On Christmas Day, Owen sat in his apartments at the Royal College of Surgeons and composed a letter to

Mantell. He acknowledged Mantell's liberal and generous conduct and thanked him for allowing him to make use of his son's rarities. Owen was probably being entirely sincere in his gratitude. The moa finds were of great benefit to him and his reputation, as they confirmed everything he'd predicted years ago, when he deduced, from just one broken bone, the former existence of the giant flightless bird. Now he wasted no time. Just a few days later he presented a paper on the moa to the Zoological Society.

Owen's gratitude didn't extend too far, however. When the Zoological Society got hold of more New Zealand bones, Owen wouldn't let Mantell see them. He kept them to himself.

The relationship between the two men seemed quite civil on the surface. They met on various social occasions, usually connected with the scientific community. Owen also spotted Mantell in the audience at his next couple of lectures, and the two men occasionally discussed fossils at the museum.

But Owen must have been slightly apprehensive when Mantell took care to make a point of showing him the wonderful belemnites he'd received from his son, Reginald, and even more so when he received a letter from Mantell explaining that he'd written a paper on the subject which would be read at the Royal Society on 23 March. Owen may well have been afraid the paper would show up his own errors. It would be unlike him not to have prepared – just in case.

On the evening of the 23rd, there was a full house at the Royal Society. That was unusual, especially as Mantell's paper wasn't about anything particularly sensational. Owen sat quietly and listened as the paper was read. Naturally, it didn't announce outright that Professor Richard Owen had made mistakes, but the fact that he had was made clear by the whole content of the paper.

When it was finished, Owen calmly got to his feet. He had never been one to admit to making a mistake, and he wasn't about to start now. Far from being defensive, he went straight on the attack. The whole topic of the paper, he declared, was too trivial to take up the members' valuable time, and should only have occupied the space of a few lines in a monthly journal. He spoke for half an hour, managing to belittle Mantell and to ridicule him and his work.

When Owen had finished, he sat down. To his immense satisfaction, he received a round of applause. He probably expected Mantell to reply to this speech, but Professor Buckland rose instead and spoke kindly in Mantell's defence. He praised his son, Reginald, for supplying the fossils which illustrated the paper, and Mantell himself for bringing his findings to the attention of the society. Perhaps this cooled things down a bit and prevented further confrontation; Mantell was now expected to reply not to Owen, but to Buckland, which he did with just a few words.

Owen may have appeared to have won the day, but there was a growing number of people who didn't like his high-handed and arrogant behaviour. However, that didn't matter a jot to him. Such was his standing, both professionally and socially, that the few objections to his behaviour – and to trivial errors contained in his work – didn't make any difference whatever. He was unassailable, it seemed.

Mantell
Jaws
1848

MANTELL MAY WELL have been sorry he'd ever let Owen set eyes on Walter's moa bones, but he was overjoyed to find that there had been a change in his son's fortunes.

The letters from New Zealand over the past year or so had become more and more despairing, until Walter wrote that he was penniless and had no prospects of a job. Apart from sending more money, Mantell tried desperately to put Walter out of his mind. At such an impossible distance, he thought, *"I know not how to rescue him."*

Then one day a quickly scrawled note was delivered, in which Walter said he was off on an expedition. He was now a moa hunter! He'd heard rumours from the New Zealand Maori people that the gigantic bird wasn't extinct at all – several people knew someone who knew someone who had actually seen one. Walter knew the

120

Maori had hunted the birds for food, and to make weapons and fish hooks from their bones. He just hoped they hadn't hunted them to extinction.

If Walter could find a moa, he said, he would be famous across the world. He could exhibit the giant bird to the public, and make masses of money. The results of his search so far were the tremendous fossil finds he'd already sent to his father. But now came the icing on the cake – a job offer which involved travelling with, and advising, the New Zealand governor and his surveyor. No doubt Walter planned, while moving around the country, to take every opportunity to track down the moa – if it existed. And Mantell was confident that if there was a moa anywhere, Walter would bring it back.

But it was doubtful if even this good news could take Mantell's mind off his own physical suffering, and off the humiliation he'd suffered at the hands of Professor Owen over his belemnite paper. Mantell knew his paper proved without doubt that Owen had made mistakes in the description and naming of his fossils. He also knew that Owen, who was known for being unwilling to admit to errors, was going to be pretty unhappy about it, to say the least. But Mantell had taken the precaution of forewarning him about the paper, and even showing him the actual belemnites he was writing about, and so never dreamed he would be the victim of such a vicious attack. He hadn't even given a thought to the unusually large number of people present.

Then he'd had to endure half an hour of what he described as Owen's *"most virulent attack"*. As if that wasn't humiliation enough, to his disgust and dismay a number of people actually clapped the man. Mantell was ever grateful for Buckland's response and kind words about him and Reginald, not least because it meant he didn't have to make a reply to the loathsome man who'd just made mincemeat of him. At least Mantell was able to leave the meeting with his dignity intact and his head high. Inwardly he was seething. Although he frequently found Owen's behaviour despicable, he had always held the man's professionalism in high regard; he had even given him the fossils his poor son Walter had so painstakingly collected, and this was the result. *"I came home to my desolate hearth, suffering in mind and body,"* he wrote, and resolved never to trust Owen's outward behaviour, and to keep well clear of him in future.

For years, Gideon Mantell had nursed a dream. He wanted to find an *Iguanodon* jaw with teeth still attached. Georges Cuvier, nearly 25 years ago, had advised him to do exactly that. Just as Owen knew Walter's moa jaw would unlock the secrets of the mysterious gigantic bird, so an *Iguanodon* jaw, complete with teeth, would provide proof that Mantell's discovery was indeed the giant herbivorous reptile he'd envisaged.

He'd searched in vain and, when ill health prevented him digging for fossils, he'd paid others what he could afford, to keep a look out. A substantial reward was promised for the elusive jaw, and an exciting find made at the end of 1847 had made Mantell even more desperate to get his hands on one. He'd asked some Isle of Wight fishermen to collect fossils for him, and one package they sent contained some bones and teeth, all from an old *Iguanodon*. One tooth seemed to be in near-perfect condition, scarcely worn away at all: *"the most beautiful I have ever seen"*. This, to Mantell, was proof that the *Iguanodon*'s teeth were constantly replaced, just like those of modern-day crocodiles, and that a young tooth like this one didn't necessarily come from a young animal – it could just as easily come from an old *Iguanodon*. This tooth was so perfect that Mantell's resolve weakened and, in spite of all their differences, he couldn't wait to show it to Professor Owen, the author of the ultimate book on teeth, *Odontography*. Owen was suitably impressed, declaring it was worth a 50-mile trip to see it.

However, Mantell still dreamed of finding more teeth, but this time attached to the jaw of an *Iguanodon*. Then, one spring day in 1848, a box was delivered to his home in Chester Square. It came from someone he'd never met, Captain Lambart Brickenden, who was the present owner of the quarry near Cuckfield where the first *Iguanodon* bones had been found. Captain Brickenden was also interested in geology, and he was sending his latest find to Gideon Mantell, in the hope that he would identify and describe it for him.

Mantell was astounded and thrilled when he opened the box to discover a section of the lower jaw of an *Iguanodon*, over 50 centimetres long. Sadly, there were no fully grown, worn-down teeth – just empty sockets. But to Mantell's delight, he found two baby teeth, still attached. These tiny, new teeth were replacements for big, old teeth. This is exactly the process in crocodiles today – new teeth are always growing below old ones, ready to push them out. After all these years, here was the proof he'd sought that the *Iguanodon* was a reptile.

Mantell took the jaw to the British Museum and compared it with those of other animals, proving to his and others' satisfaction that the *Iguanodon* was a reptile and that it was herbivorous – they could tell that from the type of teeth and the way they were worn down.

Mantell desperately wanted to own the jaw and wrote to Captain Brickenden offering in exchange for it a complete set of his own works. The captain agreed. If only he'd known, Mantell would have gladly parted with a lot more than a few books to own this fossil he'd waited nearly 25 years to find. Eleven days after first laying eyes on it, Mantell received a letter confirming the jaw was his, and a friendship with Brickenden began which would last until Mantell's death.

Though in poor health again, the thrill of having the jaw at last kept Mantell going, and he slaved away writing a paper on the *Iguanodon*'s jaws and teeth, ready for the meeting of the Royal Society on 25 May. A week beforehand he took the jaw to the Royal Society to exhibit it to members in the library. It was a miserable occasion. There was far more interest in the latest news of foreign affairs. Hardly anybody looked at the jaw or was interested in what Mantell had to say. He was really fed up, writing in his journal:

The trouble and fatigue were thrown away; and I was so ill that I ought to have been in bed.

In spite of feeling unwell, Mantell was proud to deliver his paper at last, and to let the world see his *Iguanodon* jaw – a first for science. He announced his recent findings, and also his latest estimate of the size of the *Iguanodon*'s head – probably an enormous 1.2 metres long. He could no longer agree with Professor Owen's estimate of just 75 centimetres.

Reading the paper in his weak state exhausted Mantell. And then Professor Owen rose to his feet. It was like the terrible aftermath of the belemnite paper all over again.

This time, Owen had another crushing blow to deliver. Dr Mantell was wrong, he told the audience. The fossil they saw before them was certainly not the first *Iguanodon* jaw known to science. Another specimen, smaller but more complete than this one, had been found at Horsham, in Sussex. Owen said he already had a drawing of it, and would be receiving the jaw itself very soon. When he came to describe it, he promised, his findings would reveal that not all of Dr Mantell's deductions were correct.

Mantell must have been shocked to the core. Again, Professor Owen seemed to be doing his best to outshine him. Naming the dinosaurs had in itself been devastating. Why, after all Mantell's years of painstaking work on the *Iguanodon*, was Owen seeking to outdo him yet again. Did the man have to take *everything* from him?

Owen
The Royal Medal
1848–1849

RICHARD OWEN HAD MANAGED to confound Mantell with a jaw he had never actually seen. It did exist, though. It had been found by George Bax Holmes, who'd supplied Owen with good fossils in the past, particularly specimens of the *Iguanodon*. Holmes still had it.

The jaw was from a young *Iguanodon*, and there wasn't anything to be learned from it which Mantell hadn't already discovered. Maybe Owen knew that. At any rate, he was extremely keen to get a little more information about Mantell's jaw. A few weeks later, he talked Holmes into meeting Mantell at the British Museum. Holmes was to get a good look at Mantell's jaw, make notes, and report back with all the details.

Holmes failed in his spying mission. He got nothing out of Mantell. Owen was clearly disappointed, as his next move, which he probably hated having to make, was to write to Mantell and ask him to kindly supply the information he required. It's almost certain that Mantell ignored this request.

The enmity between the two men was growing. Richard Owen was not one to let anyone outshine him. He was the one who had shown that the giant fossil land reptiles were, literally, in a class of their own. He had named the dinosaurs. They were his, and the glory was his, and that's the way he intended things to stay. No country doctor was going to eclipse him.

Owen had a vision. He'd never forgotten his visit to Cuvier's National Museum of Natural History in Paris. A whole museum devoted solely to natural history! At the moment, the main British natural history collection was housed in the British Museum: a small part of a greater whole.

His vision was for a British museum of natural history. It would be a grand place, a huge building, the envy of the world. Every collection of importance would be housed there. Perhaps they could begin, Owen suggested, by removing the British Museum exhibits (which included Gideon Mantell's collection) and bringing them under the wing of the Royal College of Surgeons, alongside the Hunterian Museum. Of course, he would expect to be in charge of this new combined collection.

Mentioning his vision in high places was the obvious thing to do, so Owen went straight to the top, to the

Prime Minister, pointing out that his branch of science hadn't had any financial support from the state for 39 years, and telling him, *"I would gladly devote the years that may be spared me in systematically arranging and expounding ... such a proposed worthy national collection."*

Owen's letter interested the Prime Minister, who invited him to discuss it further at Downing Street. Owen took the opportunity to press home the fact that the scheme would need government funding if it was to be done properly.

He came away with no definite assurances, but he had set the ball rolling. Superintending the combined fossil collections of the British Museum would at last virtually give Owen a free hand with Mantell's collection. This was definitely a project to be worked on.

But although Owen was looking to his future, he was as busy as ever with all sorts of commitments. He was involved in several public services, spending a lot of time on various organizations intended to improve conditions in sewage, slaughterhouses and public health generally. He was still giving the Hunterian lectures – a duty of the Hunterian professor – but as experienced as he now was, Owen never became complacent about them. He was always concerned that he was pitching his material at the right level for the audience. When a distinguished scientist commented that he couldn't quite follow everything in the lecture he'd just attended, Owen pondered on *"how necessary it is to address oneself to the least informed"*.

The moa – of which he was very proud – continued to occupy him. He was bitterly disappointed when the Governor of New Zealand, who'd been collecting moa bones for Owen, wrote to say his house had caught fire, and practically everything had been destroyed, including a complete moa skeleton – the largest then known. Owen had nothing so complete, but he caused a minor sensation when he had his photograph taken alongside a reconstructed moa leg. The picture showed a tall, dark Professor Owen, his eyes large and piercing, posing with one hand on the moa's thigh bone. The top of the bone was level with the crown of Owen's head. And that was only the moa's *leg*. What he would have given for one of those complete skeletons!

There were more minor clashes between Owen and Mantell. For instance, Owen had identified a creature which he called *Cetiosaurus* as being related to the crocodiles, and described it as probably a marine reptile. But when Mantell got hold of the sacrum of a *Cetiosaurus*, he was able to score over Professor Owen. This was no marine reptile – it was a dinosaur. The fused sacrum was what set dinosaurs apart from other reptiles, and Professor Owen had been the one to identify that characteristic. It must have really grated when Mantell used Owen's own research against him to prove him wrong.

Never one to take things lying down, Owen was now about to use his influence to make a further attack on his ailing enemy. The Royal Medal, the most prestigious prize in science, was due to be awarded. Mantell was nominated for his paper on the *Iguanodon*, which incorporated the recent discoveries from his study of the jaw. Another candidate was a man called Forbes, for his work on glacier ice.

Richard Owen was present on each of the three occasions the committee met to decide who would get the highly regarded medal. He did his best to persuade the committee that Mantell shouldn't have it. Physical geography, he insisted – and therefore the glacier work – was a far more worthy subject. When this opinion didn't have much effect, he started to pick holes in Mantell's work, saying it was just plain unworthy of such high honour. Owen singled out Mantell's work on the *Iguanodon* jaw in particular for severe criticism. The clash over the jaws was clearly still a sore point. He spoke up for Forbes, and managed to put the committee, as a whole, off Mantell.

On 16 November 1849, the final meeting was held. Owen again stuck out for Forbes, and never let up on his disparagement of Mantell. He must have been a very happy and satisfied man when the council voted and reached their decision.

Forbes, the glacier man, was to be their recommendation. There would be no Royal Medal for Gideon Mantell.

Mantell

"Audacious Falsehoods"

1848–1849

OWEN'S SHATTERING REVELATION, that he already had a better *Iguanodon* jaw, must have sapped what reserves of strength Mantell had left. On many a night he was reduced to taking opium to quell his pain, and even to inhaling chloroform which, he wrote, *"made me insensible for half an hour, when the spasms in the nerves of my thighs came on as bad as ever"*. This was misery enough, without being hounded by Owen.

Mantell was still smarting from the meeting in the British Museum with George Bax Holmes. He knew without doubt that Owen had sent this *"sly"* man, as he called him, to find out as much as he could about the jaw. Mantell also maintained that Holmes had obtained his jaw *after* Captain Brickenden had found the one Mantell now owned, not before, as Owen claimed. And then to receive a letter from Owen actually asking for the information he'd worked hard to extract from his own specimen; it was disgraceful. *"The designing effrontery of this request is too obvious even to me!"* wrote Mantell. Again, he vowed to avoid Owen in future and commented that *"it is very sad thus to be compelled to become as reserved and selfish as the characters I despise"*.

Just after Owen's letter arrived, Dr Rule called unexpectedly at Mantell's home. This was the man who had brought to England the original broken femur bone belonging, as Owen had so brilliantly deduced, to a giant flightless bird. Dr Rule, who was unaware that most of the fossils Mantell had ever owned were now in the British Museum, had called to see his collection of moa bones.

But Dr Rule did give Mantell his own version of the day he handed the moa bone to Owen. Rule insisted he had told Owen the bone was from a bird. So Owen had not made the terrific, imaginative deduction completely unaided! He'd known before he'd even examined it that the bone was from a bird. Yet he'd allowed everyone to fall at his feet in admiration of his brilliance. Mantell was stunned by the eminent professor's *"audacious falsehoods"*. He truly didn't know what to expect next.

Not only that, Owen had also described the fossil, scientifically, without Rule's knowledge. The doctor would certainly not have been in a position to allow that, as he had, he said, already sold it to a Bristol man for £3; it would have been for the purchaser to decide who should have the benefit of it.

Mantell may have been tempted to make his knowledge public, but he stuck to his principles, and did not.

Meanwhile, Mantell's friend, Captain Brickenden, who lived quite close to Holmes, visited him so that he could examine the smaller jaw himself. While there, he made some drawings, which he gave to Mantell. The jaw, which Owen maintained was superior to Mantell's, was clearly from a very young *Iguanodon*. Mantell's was three times the size! To his enormous relief, the drawings showed nothing that could be added to his description of his own *Iguanodon* jaw, and they didn't affect anything he'd said in any respect. This time Owen couldn't shoot holes in his paper. And for once, Mantell had something Owen didn't have. He could rest easy, sure that whatever knowledge Owen might glean from Holmes's jaw, it wouldn't be anything he, Mantell, hadn't already described.

Mantell must have felt all his work and hardships had been worthwhile when he heard, in October 1849, that he'd been nominated for the Royal Medal. When it was announced that Forbes's glacier paper had been put in the same category as his, he was quietly confident, confiding in his journal, *"What a farce! The only real geological or palaeontological papers are mine..."* After all his setbacks, his broken marriage and near-bankruptcy; in spite of losing his collection, and his health, and of having to endure the enmity of one of the most powerful and influential scientists of the day, he was to be presented with science's highest honour!

His dismay must have been great when he heard from a friend – off the record – that the committee had recommended the Royal Medal should go to Forbes. But dismay must have been totally overshadowed by disgust and frustration when he was told Owen was behind the decision. The professor hadn't just campaigned on Forbes's behalf. He had actively campaigned against Mantell.

Mantell could hardly believe Owen had described his scientific papers as unworthy, when he himself had been awarded the Royal Medal for his error-ridden belemnite paper. Owen had even accused Mantell of being a collector who just dug up fossils and let others do the professional work of describing them. Mantell must have hit the roof to hear of such a remark from a man who, to the best of his knowledge, had never found a fossil of his own in his life.

Mantell's fury at the injustice seems to have given him strength. Two days later he wrote to Buckland, now the Dean of Westminster, to protest strongly about the decision and its circumstances. Buckland replied saying he would do everything in his power to make sure the decision was reconsidered fairly. A further two days later, Mantell delivered a letter in which he told the committee he felt justice hadn't been done and asked if they would please reconsider their decision. Then he tried hard to put the whole thing out of his mind and busied himself labelling specimens and writing letters.

Mantell's persistence was rewarded when he learned the Royal Society were organizing a special meeting of the committee to think again about the medal. Privately, he insisted that the fact they were having the meeting at all was enough. He wasn't bothered about the medal itself, but, he wrote, "*it would have been dastardly tamely to submit to such gross injustice*".

Meanwhile, Buckland called to spend a couple of hours with Mantell and told him he was writing a strong letter recommending he should get the medal.

On the following Monday, Owen attended the special meeting and, according to a friend of Mantell's, held back nothing in his efforts to stop the medal going to his enemy. As Mantell wrote later, "*What a pity that a man of so much talent and acquirement should be so dastardly and envious.*" But friends such as Charles Lyell spoke for Mantell and although Buckland wasn't there, his letter was read out.

Justice was done. The committee voted to recommend awarding the Royal Medal to Gideon Mantell. He would hear on the following Friday if the council of the Royal Society would act on that recommendation.

Owen

A Straightforward Request
1849–1850

OWEN MUST HAVE BEEN LIVID when his attempts to block Mantell's chances of the Royal Medal went wrong. He must also have been rather shaken that, apart from his own, there had been only one other vote against Mantell. People he'd thought would respect his judgement and vote with him had suddenly changed sides. Professor Buckland had written a letter praising Mantell to the skies, and Charles Lyell had come armed with a sheaf of notes which he kept referring to when speaking up for his friend. How dare these people go against Professor Richard Owen's recommendations! He was the greatest anatomist of the age – everyone knew it.

When the medal was formally presented to Mantell, Owen sat directly opposite him, glaring with his penetrating eyes. As the evening wore on, he noticed Mantell was becoming paler, and was clearly in some discomfort. Owen had to watch the other scientists congratulating the winner who, well before the meeting ended, pulled himself to his feet and went home.

A couple of weeks later, at a meeting of the council of the Royal Society, Owen was greeting a few acquaintances with a handshake, when he turned to be confronted by Gideon Mantell. He offered his hand and calmly said that it gave him the greatest pleasure to see Mantell there. Mantell kept his own hands firmly by his side, gave a small bow, and turned away. This, in front of so many fellow members, was a great embarrassment for Owen.

But all the grumbling Mantell must have been doing to his friends about the fight he'd had for the Royal Medal would have been so much water off a duck's back to Richard Owen. Not being one to shrink from criticizing others, sometimes unfairly, he'd made more than one enemy in his rise to the top. Mantell was virtually a broken man. The country doctor might have achieved the recognition and respect that the Royal Medal conferred, but what else did he have going for him? A pitiably small collection, compared with the one he'd lost, a failed marriage, money problems. On top of all that, he was constantly dogged by health problems.

In October 1850, Owen was in the final stages of preparing a book on British fossil reptiles. This was to be the last word on the subject – the book everyone would refer to. It would contain all the current knowledge available. It had to be illustrated, of course, and Owen wanted the best.

He decided he needed to use some drawings which had already been published in the journal of the Royal Society, and applied to the council for permission to reproduce them. The illustrations he wanted to use were, he said, of specimens which had been described by him in his 1842 "Report on British Fossil Reptiles".

The council members were unaware that several of the illustrations in question were actually from Gideon Mantell's own papers on the *Iguanodon* and the *Hylaeosaurus*. Richard Owen didn't bother to inform them of that, but let them think he was entitled to use the illustrations. It all seemed perfectly in order to the council members, and they saw no reason to refuse such a straightforward request. On 24 October, it was recorded that Professor Owen's request should be granted.

One of the illustrations in question was of the *Iguanodon* jaw which Mantell had got from Captain Brickenden. It's amazing that Owen had the nerve to include that one. How could it possibly have been included in his 1842 report when it hadn't even been discovered until years later – and so recently, too?

Mantell soon heard about this and, a week later, there was a Royal Society council meeting, when he was able to say his piece. However, all the council members present said they were confident that the illustrations in question were Professor Owen's. When the council met

139

on 14 November, Owen blithely repeated that the illustrations were from specimens described by him in his 1842 report.

A fortnight later, at another meeting of the council, Mantell delivered his body blow in the shape of a letter. Apart from a very few instances, he said, none of the other illustrations in dispute could possibly be from specimens Owen had described in his "Report on British Fossil Reptiles", because they hadn't been discovered until later. There was no way Owen could have described the *Iguanodon* jaw, for instance, because no such jaw had been found at that time.

Then Mantell produced the proof. He'd written to Captain Brickenden asking him exactly when and where he had found the *Iguanodon* jaw. Had Brickenden ever let it out of his possession or even out of his house until he sent it to Mantell? The reply was produced for the benefit of the council, and of Professor Owen. Captain Brickenden's response proved Owen could not possibly have had the *Iguanodon* jaw in his possession at the time he published his "Report on British Fossil Reptiles", and nor could he have had any opportunity of seeing it before Dr Mantell presented it to the Royal Society in 1848.

For once, Owen had nothing to say in his defence. There was no excuse. He spoke coolly and calmly, murmuring an apology. Professor Richard Owen had been humbled and humiliated by Mantell in front of the senior members of the Royal Society.

Crystal Palace
1850–1851

THE ACCOLADE OF the Royal Medal should have been one of the highest points in Gideon Mantell's life. This was the recognition by his peers which he'd longed for, right back in the early years when he'd had an inkling that one day he might make his name. Instead, the joy was ruined by the controversy. He couldn't even take pleasure in the actual presentation of the medal, when, as he wrote, *"Owen sat opposite me and looked the picture of malevolence."*

He constantly wondered why Owen behaved as he did. The man had everything going for him. He had free access to the whole of Mantell's major collection. Mantell felt Owen was jealously trying to rob him of every last thing, still trying to enhance his own reputation at Mantell's expense, still trying to be "the dinosaur man". He would even have attempted to take the credit for the *Iguanodon* jaw if Mantell hadn't stopped him. At least Mantell had the small satisfaction of refusing the handshake Owen offered.

When he wrote to thank Captain Brickenden for his support, and to explain why he'd needed it, Mantell added:

> *It is indeed lamentable that a man so highly gifted, and one who has been overpaid and overpraised for all he has done, should be cursed with such a jealous and monopolizing spirit.*

Mantell was possibly unaware until recently that Owen was beginning to cause trouble elsewhere, and was falling out with all sorts of people. For instance, Mantell wasn't the only Royal Medal candidate to suffer at Owen's hands. When a physician, Robert Lee, called to congratulate Mantell on his success, he confided that Owen had prevented him receiving the same award. However, perhaps Mantell had suffered rather more than most, and he must have wondered, as time went on, when Owen was going to stop his sniping and leave him alone. He didn't have the energy for confrontations. He was over 60 now, tired, and suffering a great deal. Visits still had to be made to his regular patients in Clapham, and he would often come home completely exhausted, only to spend a sleepless night tossing about in pain. Chloroform gave him short periods of relief but made him feel so ill he resolved not to take any more.

In the early part of 1851, it was clear that Mantell's health was failing badly. He had already written his will, with various bequests, leaving most of his possessions to Reginald, the son who had stayed closest to him. Reginald was to have whatever specimens, books and other items he wanted, and the rest was to be sold – to the British Museum, Mantell hoped.

Now, aware he probably didn't have much time left, he wrote a letter to his nephew, outlining his wishes in the event of his death. The letter was to be opened as soon as Mantell died. He asked that there should be a post-mortem on his body, and if anything of medical interest was to be discovered, he would like the appropriate part or parts to be given to the Hunterian Museum at the Royal College of Surgeons.

Mantell wrote that his funeral was to be in the early morning, and as plain and quiet as possible. Unsurprisingly, he wished to be buried in the cemetery at West Norwood, next to his beloved Hannah, for whom he'd never ceased to mourn.

But life went on, and the highlight of 1851 was the Great Exhibition in London's Hyde Park. The magnificent Crystal Palace, built to house the exhibits, had been under construction since August the previous year, and the grand opening took place on 1 May. The whole scheme had been Prince Albert's brainchild, and Mantell would almost certainly have heard insider details of the plans. At any rate, he was entranced by the exhibition, writing, *"It is quite overpowering. I cannot express the effect it has left upon my mind."*

As a geologist, Mantell was thrilled to see a beautiful Austrian opal and *"a fine mass of quartz-rock with rich veins of gold"*, which was a product of the recent Californian gold rush. The exhibition displayed goods from all over the world, and he was especially intrigued by the different watches and clocks, machinery from France, and exquisite works of art and craft from many nations. There was so much to see that Mantell visited again and again, and was there at the closing ceremony five and a half months later.

Shortly afterwards, he came to the end of eight months' extremely hard work on a book he'd been writing, called *Petrifactions and their Teachings*. Mantell reckoned working on it night after night had almost finished him off. *Petrifactions* was a handbook to the fossils in the British Museum, and was to be his final book. Owen, naturally, featured in it, and Mantell peppered his references to the great anatomist with a few satisfying digs.

Mantell was becoming concerned that Owen, still at the Hunterian Museum, might be moving in on the British Museum. In the previous August, Mantell's friend Charles König had had a bad fall on his own front doorstep, and died soon afterwards. Mantell was saddened. He'd respected König and had been fond of him, even dedicating his current book to him. König's death left vacant his position as Superintendent of Geology at the British Museum. Mantell knew Owen hoped to get the job. He himself supported another candidate, Owen's friend, George Waterhouse.

Owen was livid with Charles Lyell (who openly supported Waterhouse) and wrote a vicious attack on him. Mantell was quietly satisfied about this. He reckoned Lyell, who hadn't seemed to understand what it was like to cross swords with the man, *"will now understand the real character of Owen!"*

Mantell himself would not escape unscathed if Owen got the job. He told a friend he'd probably have to stay away from the British Museum if Owen was in charge – which meant staying away from his own collection, too.

Towards the end of 1851, Captain Brickenden was about to announce the discovery of an intriguing little fossil reptile skeleton found near Elgin in Scotland by his brother-in-law, Patrick Duff. He sent the manuscript of his paper to Mantell, who realized this fossil was older than any reptile fossil uncovered so far. It was an enormously important find.

Mantell told Brickenden the reptile ought to be described in more detail, and it would be best if, when the paper was read, the skeleton could be there at the same time for the scientists to see. Could Patrick Duff and Brickenden let him have it, he wondered? He would be happy to do the extra work and present a joint paper.

Brickenden agreed, and Patrick Duff consented to send the fossil to his brother George in London. Meanwhile, Mantell had shown Brickenden's drawings to Charles Lyell, who also became wildly excited.

With full permission, Mantell wrote his section about the reptile within a very few days and sent the paper to the Geological Society, where he was scheduled to read it two weeks later, on 17 December 1851. He'd already decided on the creature's name, which was to be *Telerpeton*, meaning "oldest reptile".

On the evening of the meeting, clutching the reptile skeleton, which was only about 15 centimetres long, Mantell sat listening to a paper on temperature and climate. He found it interesting enough, but must have been bursting to get on and read his own paper. His excitement turned to impatience as the speaker droned on and on. When he'd finished, there was the usual discussion afterwards. Mantell was dismayed to see it was gone 11 o'clock by this time. Sure enough, even though his paper had been announced, it was postponed.

A few people were interested enough to have a good look at the specimen before they went home, and one of these was Professor Owen. Mantell noted in his journal that Owen examined it carefully, pored over Mantell's anatomical drawings, and then left; one eyewitness reported him looking absolutely furious. No doubt Mantell felt a little apprehensive, but he couldn't imagine what could possibly have upset Owen quite so much.

The Telerpeton Affair

1851-1852

WHILE MANTELL'S HEALTH deteriorated and every bit of strain told on him, Richard Owen, though never one to forget, simply moved on. He'd been showered with honours from all directions through the year. A knighthood was offered by the King of Prussia; he was invited to sit on the committee for the Great Exhibition; and he attended meetings with Prince Albert at Buckingham Palace. Owen soon found himself at formal court events, and decided it was high time he had a proper outfit made for such occasions. He and Caroline consulted a court tailor, and ended up with *"a very handsome and elegant attire"*, as he told his sister. It had *"bright steel buttons, buckles, sword, etc., and a white satin waistcoat with rich flowers embroidered"*. Topped off with a cocked hat and long lace cravat, he was highly pleased with what he saw in the mirror when it was complete. What a long way he had come, this trader's son.

The little setback over the matter of Mantell's illustrations hadn't fazed Owen at all. He had far more important things to think about. It's likely he felt fairly confident that he'd soon get König's position as superintendent of the British Museum geology collection. After all, certain influential people had suggested he go for it and, with his combined abilities, experience and qualifications, he'd surely eclipse everyone else. It looked almost like a foregone conclusion. With his standing and his connections, who was better placed?

A rumour went round that Professor Owen had been given the job. When the other candidate, George Waterhouse, heard it, he more or less gave up. But then, on 22 December, Waterhouse was told the position was his! It was said that Professor Owen had withdrawn his application. Rumours suggested he'd pulled out because he'd realized he wasn't going to get the post, and couldn't bear to be seen to lose. But Owen quickly scotched those by saying he hadn't written a letter of withdrawal at all; he'd actually written to recommend George Waterhouse. We don't know exactly what happened. Perhaps he did sense defeat. Perhaps the extra money, a mere £50 a year, wasn't enough.

Meanwhile, there was the problem of the so-called *Telerpeton*. Owen had indeed been angry at the meeting of the Geological Society when Mantell displayed the ancient skeleton. Within three days, on 20 December,

Owen announced in the *Literary Gazette* that Patrick Duff had intended him to describe and name the reptile. This he now did, in print, calling it *Leptopleuron lacertinum*, which means "slender-ribbed reptile".

Although Mantell immediately got on to the newspaper editor saying this was not true, it seems there was something to it after all. Patrick Duff had sent his brother George details and a drawing of the fossil, and originally he did ask George to let Professor Owen have them. But then Brickenden had told Patrick that Mantell was interested and wanted to see the actual specimen. Patrick sent the skeleton with the instruction that any of the top London scientists could look at it. George wrote back, saying Owen, Mantell and Lyell all wanted it, so Patrick must choose who was to have it. The decision was made: if it hadn't actually been promised to Owen, then Patrick wished Gideon Mantell to have it first.

Owen believed he had the right to keep his name for the specimen because, as far as he was concerned, he had been the first to scientifically describe it. But Mantell had previously made a cast of the fossil for Charles Lyell. This had been used in a lecture at roughly the same time as Mantell had been due to read his and Brickenden's joint paper. Lyell, had, on this occasion, announced Mantell's name, *Telerpeton elginense*. So, the fossil had been described and named before Owen's letter to the newspaper in which he proposed his own name.

And then Mantell read his *Telerpeton* paper at the next meeting of the Geological Society on 7 January, 1852.

Afterwards, the president announced that although the paper had only just been read, the title had been declared by the chairman at the December meeting, and therefore it took precedence over anyone else's description of *Telerpeton*. Mantell's description, and the name he gave the creature, was to be the official one.

One wonderful morning, a letter arrived for Owen bearing the royal coat of arms. It was signed by CB Phipps, on behalf of Queen Victoria, and began,

> *I have been commanded by the Queen to inform you that, a house upon Kew Green having become vacant by the death of the King of Hanover, Her Majesty is happy in being able to offer this house as a residence for you.*

Mr Phipps referred to him as being one of science's *"chief ornaments and most distinguished members"*.

Owen was thrilled, but there was a drawback. The house needed to have a lot done to it. How the King of Hanover managed in it, we can't be sure, because Phipps's letter went on to say that part of the house would have to be pulled down, as it wasn't fit to be repaired.

So, here was an excellent reason for Owen to – as he put it in a letter to his sister – *"push the British Museum question no further"*. Maybe this was the point at which he decided that a magnificent – well, fairly magnificent –

new home in Kew was enough to make him give up his application for König's post. After all, if he was working at the British Museum, it would be essential for him to live in London. Perhaps he did withdraw and recommend Waterhouse for good reasons, rather than – as Mantell was convinced – because he was certain to lose.

Without question, Owen told his sister, it had been a wonderful year, and now, after all the success came what he called the *"solid pudding"*. A beautiful home, courtesy of Her Majesty, would give lasting benefit and enormous pleasure to him and his family. It was of far more practical use than Prussian knighthoods, and a huge honour.

When Owen arrived one day to look over the late King of Hanover's house, he was disconcerted when the caretaker wouldn't let him in. He protested that he needed to sort out what furniture was needed, and what would go where, but the caretaker said he'd just have to put off his plans for a while.

It seemed there was no certainty at the time that the house actually belonged to Queen Victoria, which must have taken some of the shine off for Owen. He'd been presented with a house, but part of it needed to be done up, and part needed pulling down. To cap it all, he wasn't even sure who it belonged to.

Then he heard from a friend about another house – one that definitely did belong to the Queen – in Richmond Park. No one was living in it at present. Owen went to see Sheen Lodge, and decided it was perfect for him.

But how do you tell the Queen you're very grateful for her present, but you'd like to change it, please? Owen pulled the one string he had. He set off for Osborne House on the Isle of Wight to put the problem to Prince Albert. Owen chatted politely with Albert about the layout of the gardens at Osborne, no doubt impatiently, and then asked if it could be fixed for him to have Sheen Lodge instead of the Kew house.

Albert thought the house was too small; *"merely a cottage"*, as he described it, but he agreed to speak to the Queen on Owen's behalf. She was quite happy with the arrangement, and soon another letter came from Phipps, saying, *"Allow me heartily to congratulate you, and to wish you every enjoyment in your new abode."*

By the middle of 1852, Owen was comfortably settled in the "cottage", which was in fact a large, many-gabled house with tall chimneys, in a wonderful rural setting. He and Caroline stayed in Sheen Lodge for the rest of their lives, in great comfort, and loved it.

"Oh! it is Almost Unbearable"

1852

GIDEON MANTELL COULD never bring himself to believe Owen had any other motive for "withdrawing" his application for König's job than fear of defeat. When he read that Owen had informed the Athenaeum that he hadn't sent a withdrawal at all, but a recommendation for Waterhouse, he recalled how Owen had actively canvassed for support among their mutual acquaintances. To Mantell it was perfectly clear that he desperately wanted the job. Owen's words were an *"atrocious falsehood"*, he wrote furiously in his journal. *"What lamentable turpitude* [wickedness]."

For his own part, Mantell was feeling extremely satisfied following the *Telerpeton* affair. After all the quarrelling and bad feeling generated by the existence of this tiny creature, he had finally been able to read his paper at the Geological Society on 7 January. Above all,

Mantell knew that his name for it, *Telerpeton*, was now official.

But feelings of triumph were dwarfed by the suffering Mantell was going through. *"Oh! it is almost unbearable,"* he wrote after struggling to get up one morning. He had to endure regular bouts of agonizing pains in his legs, yet was still forced to make his way to Clapham to attend his patients; money must still be earned. He seems to have had good days when he would enjoy attending meetings and lectures, but pain was always lurking. One March day, he recorded how he'd tried to deal with his pain during the previous night. *"No relief from prussic acid, liniments, fomentations, calomel and opium, hot brandy etc. all of no avail."* The amount of opium-based drugs Mantell was using had been gradually increasing for some time. He was now taking 32 times the adult dose.

Mantell found the few lectures he gave to be exhausting. This was partly the fault of his own skill and popularity. The public kept hearing of new discoveries, and must have wondered how much more there was for the scientists to unearth. They flocked to hear what Mantell had to say, and were astounded by the size of the fossils, and by the drawings that showed what the monsters might have looked like. The audience was often so fascinated by what he had to say that he'd be standing for another half an hour afterwards, answering questions, and explaining drawings and microscope exhibits.

Unexpectedly, practical relief arrived, in the form of financial recognition for the work Mantell had done. *"To my utter astonishment,"* he wrote in June, *"received a note from the Earl of Rosse* [the President of the Royal Society] *informing me that at his suggestion, the Minister, Lord Derby had offered me an annuity of £100 as an expression of respect from the Crown for my scientific labours! ... It is very gratifying in every sense."* Though immensely grateful for the welcome cash, he was slightly disappointed. Twice that sum would have meant he could move somewhere cheaper, give up his medical work, and fulfil his dream. *"I am still dreaming of a History of the Wealden,"* he wrote to a close friend. *"What a glorious volume the fauna and flora of the country of the Iguanodon would make – if I had but the means wherewithal to do it."*

Mantell badly needed this injection of cash. Many of his journal entries in the summer months of 1852 recorded his sufferings. He was miserable and lonely. His daughter, Ellen Maria, called to see him with her son one day in July. It was the first time she'd visited his home for nine years.

The gorgeous glass Crystal Palace had served its purpose and was due to be pulled down. There were many, like Mantell, who were bowled over by its beauty, and who thought it would be a sin to destroy it. He wrote of *"the almost universal desire that it should remain"*. There was a campaign to keep the building, in which Richard Owen was involved, and probably Mantell, too, as he referred in a letter to *"our"* efforts, meaning the campaigners generally. The Crystal Palace Company listened to the people and by the end of May, Mantell was delighted to hear the building was not to be destroyed. It was to be moved to Penge Hill, Sydenham, now South London, where it would stand high on a hill for over 80 years. At night, it would be visible for miles.

Mantell might have thought that was the final word on the Crystal Palace as far as he was concerned. The object had been achieved: the building had been saved. But the company had an idea. There was to be an area set aside specially to celebrate the science of geology. The idea was to display life-sized models of animals and plants of the past in their particular geological periods. Naturally, a major feature – and a terrific draw to the public – would be the magnificent giant fossil reptiles. Dinosaurs – full-size! The public would go wild for them.

The Crystal Palace Company needed someone with the appropriate scientific knowledge to oversee this high-profile project. But equally, they needed someone with the imagination to bring old bones to life, and to set them in a realistic background. Both Mantell and Owen had the necessary scientific background, but one of them had consistently striven to place the monstrous beasts in their true habitats. That man was Gideon Mantell.

On 18 August he received a visit from two members of the company, and they consulted him about the proposed geological court. Two days later, the secretary of the natural history department of the new Crystal Palace called. Mantell noted that evening in his journal:

> *I found that the plan intended to be carried out as Geology, was merely to have models of extinct animals, which were hereafter to be distributed over the building. I therefore declined the superintendance of such a scheme.*

Mantell clearly didn't think much of the idea. We don't really know what his feelings were at being asked to supervise the restoration of his beloved dinosaurs, or the real reason for his refusal. We can assume he took it as a gesture of the greatest respect, and of recognition for the knowledge gained in a lifetime of dedicated study. It must have been a moment of quiet pride and satisfaction. However, it's known he preferred proper scientific displays, using fossils, drawings and diagrams, to supposedly lifelike models – after all, how could the models be totally accurate when no one had ever seen a living beast? What colour were they, for instance?

But it's very likely that at least part of the reason Mantell refused was that he knew he couldn't do the job. He just wasn't physically strong enough, and there'd been times over the last few years when he was sure he didn't have long to live.

He was in constant, soul-destroying pain, and couldn't get about very much. *"My wretched worn-out frame still holds together – for some wise purpose,* doubtless," he wrote to a friend, *"and I must work on to the end."*

Work on to the end he did, struggling to Clapham to visit his few patients, and even lecturing, although he was unable to stand for more than a few minutes. Mantell's enthusiasm for his subject was the only thing that carried him through these trials of endurance.

For as long as he was able, Mantell continued to visit Hannah's grave in West Norwood Cemetery. On 28 September, he summoned the strength for the journey once more.

By October, everything was getting a bit too much. He had book proofs to correct; even his printer was *"now proceeding as much too fast as previously too slow"*. Around the first week of November, Mantell seems to have muddled the dates in his journal. He'd also begun sending household goods, like a pair of bronze chandeliers and some tablecloths, to his daughter Ellen. He was getting rid of his possessions.

One chill November day, Mantell was in such constant pain that he was unable to do more than sit by the fire trying to warm himself. Nothing he did brought any relief so, at eight in the evening, he decided to go to bed. Perhaps sleep, and a dose of his drugs, would bring relief.

Unsteady on his feet as he climbed the stairs, he fell. He couldn't get up, so had to crawl to his bedroom. He climbed into bed and took half of the medicine, but it had hardly any effect so, in desperation, he swallowed the rest.

Next day, the servants couldn't rouse him. He was unconscious. At three in the afternoon of 10 November, Gideon Mantell died. His suffering was at an end.

Owen

"Our British Cuvier"

1852–1854

EVEN MANTELL'S DEATH didn't put a stop to Richard Owen's enmity.

Among the obituaries which appeared soon afterwards was one in the *Literary Gazette*. It was complimentary about Mantell as a man, but highly critical of him as a scientist. It implied he wasn't particularly knowledgeable in scientific matters. The writer used Mantell's own *Iguanodon* to really put the boot in, intimating that Mantell had done little more than dig up the bones; others had done the real work. Georges Cuvier, the writer continued, had been the one to realize it was a reptile; William Clift had been the one to compare the *Iguanodon*'s teeth to the modern iguana; someone else had given it its name; and Richard Owen had identified the features which characterized it – indeed, he'd even put right Mantell's errors about the size of the creature.

Hardly anyone in the world of geology had any doubt that the author of this vicious, ill-meant obituary was none other than Professor Richard Owen. It was difficult for everyone to understand how someone so eminent, well respected and successful should feel the need to write in such a malignant way about a dead man. There was no question that the two of them had had their battles. But Mantell had never appeared to have any desire to actually harm Owen in any way. He was known to have frequently shared his findings; for instance, in handing over the bones Walter sent from New Zealand, Mantell had known they would play a good part in enhancing Owen's reputation. He had even written Owen a friendly letter, warning him not to overdo it: because of overworking, he was now *"fit for nothing ... be warned by my example,"* he wrote. But, it seemed Owen was unable to resist the opportunity for another attack.

Owen was well aware that, in most circles, his behaviour was deplored. But he was far too busy to worry about it. He had yet one more way to score. He'd now been asked to design the life-size models for the geology display at the new Crystal Palace.

Surely Owen must have felt a particular triumph as he worked on the *Iguanodon* with Benjamin Waterhouse Hawkins, the man who actually modelled them. *His* vision of the *Iguanodon* would be the one the public would see, not Mantell's. *Hylaeosaurus*, too, would be brought to life under his direction, and *Megalosaurus* – Mary Anning's plesiosaur, too.

He, Richard Owen, had named the dinosaurs. Now he would show the world exactly what they were like – without anyone interfering or arguing with him. The dinosaurs were his, and his name would be linked with them forever.

The *Iguanodon* eventually stood on four chunky legs. Mantell's vision of a beast walking on two strong hind legs, with smaller front limbs, had been tossed aside. Owen's *Iguanodon* stood four-square like a rhinoceros, as he'd always argued it did. On the end of its mighty nose would be the horn.

At Christmas time in 1853, several eminent scientists received a strange communication about an even stranger, and probably unique, event. It was a card, with a picture of a pterodactyl. Written on the wing of the pterodactyl was an invitation to a sumptuous seven-course New Year's Eve celebration dinner, to be held inside the body of – an *Iguanodon*!

When the guests gathered in the late afternoon at the Crystal Palace, they found a beautifully laid table and 21 seats set up inside the half-completed mould of the *Iguanodon* model. A few more guests sat at a side table. The less glamorous surroundings of the rest of the part-finished exhibits were disguised by an elegantly draped marquee, and the table was lit by a large chandelier.

Around the "walls", banners commemorated eminent scientists. Among those who had played a part in the discovery of dinosaurs were Buckland, Cuvier and Mantell, all of whom were now dead. Another banner bore the name of Owen, who was not only very much alive but sitting at the head of the table in the arch formed by the head of the *Iguanodon*. Drawings were made of the occasion, which appeared with a report in the *Illustrated London News*, and it would be hard to think of a more intriguing publicity stunt.

The new, permanent Crystal Palace exhibition opened in 1854. At the ceremony, Owen, as a VIP, was part of the royal party. The Crystal Palace Company chairman said in his speech:

> The restoration from a single fossil fragment of complete skeletons of creatures long since extinct ... has always been considered one of the most striking achievements of modern science. Our British Cuvier, Professor Owen, has lent us his assistance in carrying these scientific triumphs a step further and in bringing them down to popular apprehension.

There is no question that the dinosaurs were a terrific draw; the public flocked in their thousands to gaze at them. At last, they could see with their own eyes the great prehistoric beasts that scientists had painstakingly teased from a few fossilized bones. Enthusiasm for the prehistoric world mushroomed all over the globe as professional and amateur scientists, and ordinary people, searched for more specimens, seeking to find bigger and better dinosaurs. They began to feature in stories, not just in passing, as with Dickens's *Megalosaurus*, but in tales of adventure and exploration; and they have always been a popular subject for artists and illustrators.

And the scientist who had named them was the one to bring them before the eyes of the world. To the crowds thronging the Crystal Palace park, there was no doubt: Richard Owen was ... the dinosaur man.

Afterword

GIDEON MANTELL WAS BURIED, according to his wishes, next to his adored daughter, Hannah. His funeral, in West Norwood Cemetery, was the quiet affair he had asked for. There were few mourners, but that was the way he'd wanted it.

When the post-mortem was carried out, Mantell's spine was found to be badly twisted. There was no tumour or abscess. Because of the severe deformity, it was thought sufficiently interesting to be exhibited in the Hunterian Museum where it was, for a few years, in the care of Professor Richard Owen. The spine was eventually destroyed by a German bomb during the Second World War.

Mantell's son, Reginald, took what fossils and other specimens he wanted from his father's collection, and the rest were sold to the British Museum. Five years later, he had a brass plaque put on the wall of St Michael's Church, just a few metres along the High Street from Castle Place, in Lewes. It gives the year of Gideon Mantell's death incorrectly as 1853, instead of 1852.

Richard Owen resigned from the Hunterian Museum in 1856 after nearly 30 years, first as assistant, then, following the death of his father-in-law in 1849, as conservator. He joined the British Museum, where he was made the first superintendent of the natural history collections.

On a personal level, Owen's star continued to rise. He gave lectures to the royal family; he was invited to tutor the princes and princesses; he was knighted and he ruled the scientific roost for years. But it wasn't all plain sailing. Owen eventually accepted there was some form of evolution, although he still believed all creatures were based on the same basic archetype. He could not accept Charles Darwin's theory of evolution by natural selection. How could man have evolved from an ape?

When Darwin published his *On the Origin of Species* in 1859, Owen took every opportunity to attack the ideas contained in the book. This only succeeded in bringing down the wrath of the scientist Thomas Huxley, one of Darwin's allies. Huxley so despised Richard Owen that he deliberately undermined him and belittled his ideas whenever he got the chance. He took great satisfaction in damaging Owen's reputation by pointing out his mistakes. Owen suddenly found himself on the receiving end of the enmity of someone stronger than himself – Huxley was so formidable that he was known as "Darwin's bulldog".

But Owen was the one who would have a great lasting monument to his life's work. As soon as he began working at the British Museum, he started to campaign for his long-dreamed-of national museum of natural history. He plugged away at the idea for years and was eventually to see the dream realized: the British Museum (Natural History) opened in 1881 in a magnificent new building in South Kensington. It is now known as the Natural History Museum.

A bronze statue of Richard Owen, by Thomas Brock, stands in a prominent position at the head of the stairs opposite the main entrance of the museum, beyond a full-size *Diplodocus* skeleton. It would have given Owen some satisfaction to know that, in 1927, a marble statue of Darwin was moved to make way for his. Both Darwin's statue and one of Huxley are now in the museum's North Hall.

Owen died in 1892, but lived long enough to learn that he'd been wrong about the size of the *Iguanodon*'s front legs, and that Mantell had been right – it did have smaller, lighter forelimbs. He also had to accept that the horn he'd so carefully positioned on the end of the Crystal Palace *Iguanodon*'s nose was not a horn at all. It was a hard, spiked thumb – possibly used as a weapon.

There was no statue of Gideon Mantell, the first person to have any conception of a time when giant reptiles stalked the Earth. However, 148 years after his death, a monument commemorating the discovery of the *Iguanodon* was erected at Whiteman's Green in Sussex, where it all began.

The Earth still holds its secrets, but scientists who study fossil plants and animals (now known as palaeontologists) continue to uncover them and to build on the work of those great men of the nineteenth century – the discoverers of dinosaurs.

Sources and Further Reading

The Dinosaur Hunters, by Deborah Cadbury (Fourth Estate, 2000)

The Journal of Gideon Mantell, Surgeon and Geologist, edited by E Cecil Curwen (Oxford University Press, 1940)

Gideon Mantell and the Discovery of Dinosaurs, by Dennis R Dean (Cambridge University Press, 1999)

Gideon Algernon Mantell, by Sidney Spokes (John Bale, Sons & Danielsson Ltd, 1927)

The Life of Richard Owen, by The Reverend Richard Owen (John Murray, 1894)

Richard Owen: Victorian Naturalist, by Nicolaas A Rupke (Yale University Press, 1994)

The Natural History Museum Book of Dinosaurs, by Tim Gardom and Angela Milner (Carlton Books, 2001)

The Crystal Palace Dinosaurs, by Steve McCarthy and Mick Gilbert (The Crystal Palace Foundation, 1994)

The following museums also have a wealth of information about the discovery of dinosaurs:

The Natural History Museum, Cromwell Road, London, SW7 5BD www.nhm.ac.uk

Lewes Castle and Barbican House Museum, Lewes, Sussex, BN7 1YE www.sussexpast.co.uk

Crystal Palace Park Dinosaurs and Geological Time Trail, Thicket Road, Penge, London SE20 8DT Information centre 020 8778 9496

Acknowledgements

Thanks to Esme Evans and the Sussex Archaeological Society, Lewes, for access to Gideon Mantell's unpublished journal; Crystal Palace Foundation; Crystal Palace Park Rangers; Friends of West Norwood Cemetery; Polly Tucker, Assistant Archivist of the Natural History Museum, Dr Jane Clarke, Sue Watkinson, Sally and Ben Webb, Robin Williams and Chris Pluck.

Picture insert
1   Gideon Mantell © The Natural History Museum, London
2   Richard Owen © Hulton Archive/Getty Images
3   Mary Ann Mantell © The Natural History Museum, London
4   *Iguanodon* teeth © Topfoto Corporation of London/HIP

Diagram of geological strata by Michelle Hearne

Index

DOUBLE TAKE
Two sides. One story

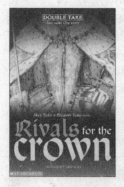

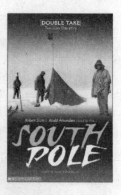

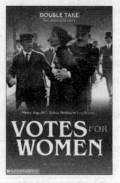

There are always two sides to every story...